Inside the Rainbow
Volume 4

Read and See Revelation 12–14

Pieter Kwant

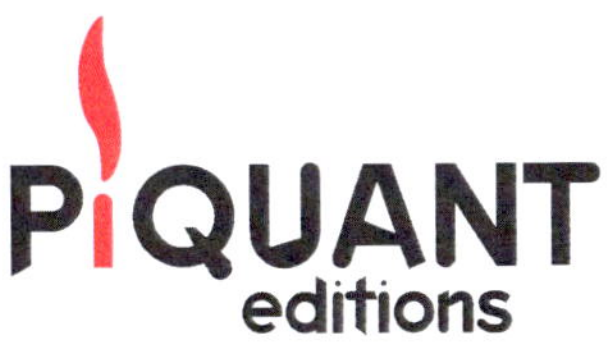

First published in Great Britain in 2025 by Piquant Editions

www.piquanteditions.com

British Library Cataloguing-in-Publication Data
A catalogue record for this book is available from the British Library

ISBN: 978-1-80329-017-1

Cover Painting: *Woman crying out in agony* (2024) by Pieter Kwant
Cover design: Projectluz.com

This book was painted and written with Elria
for

Dave & Heather, Josh & Lauren,
Barnes & Beth, Tim & Nomes,
as well as

Susie, Isla, Dougal,
Lucas, Ciara, Heidi,
Zahra, Ava,
Saoirse, Jonah and Hudson.

I dedicate Volume 4 to the memory of the Ukrainian martyrs.

"You heard me say to you, 'I am going away, and I am coming to you.' If you loved me, you would rejoice that I am going to the Father, because the Father is greater than I.
"And now I have told you this before it occurs, so that when it does occur, you may believe. I will no longer talk much with you, for the ruler of this world is coming. He has no power over me, but I do as the Father has commanded me, so that the world may know that I love the Father. Rise, let us be on our way."
John 14:25–31

"In her misfortunes the church is always bringing forth Christ through her members, and the dragon is always seeking to devour the one who is being born … the church is the body of Christ, because she is always bringing forth members of Christ."
St Caesarius, a fifth-century saint from Gaul in France (2011:85)

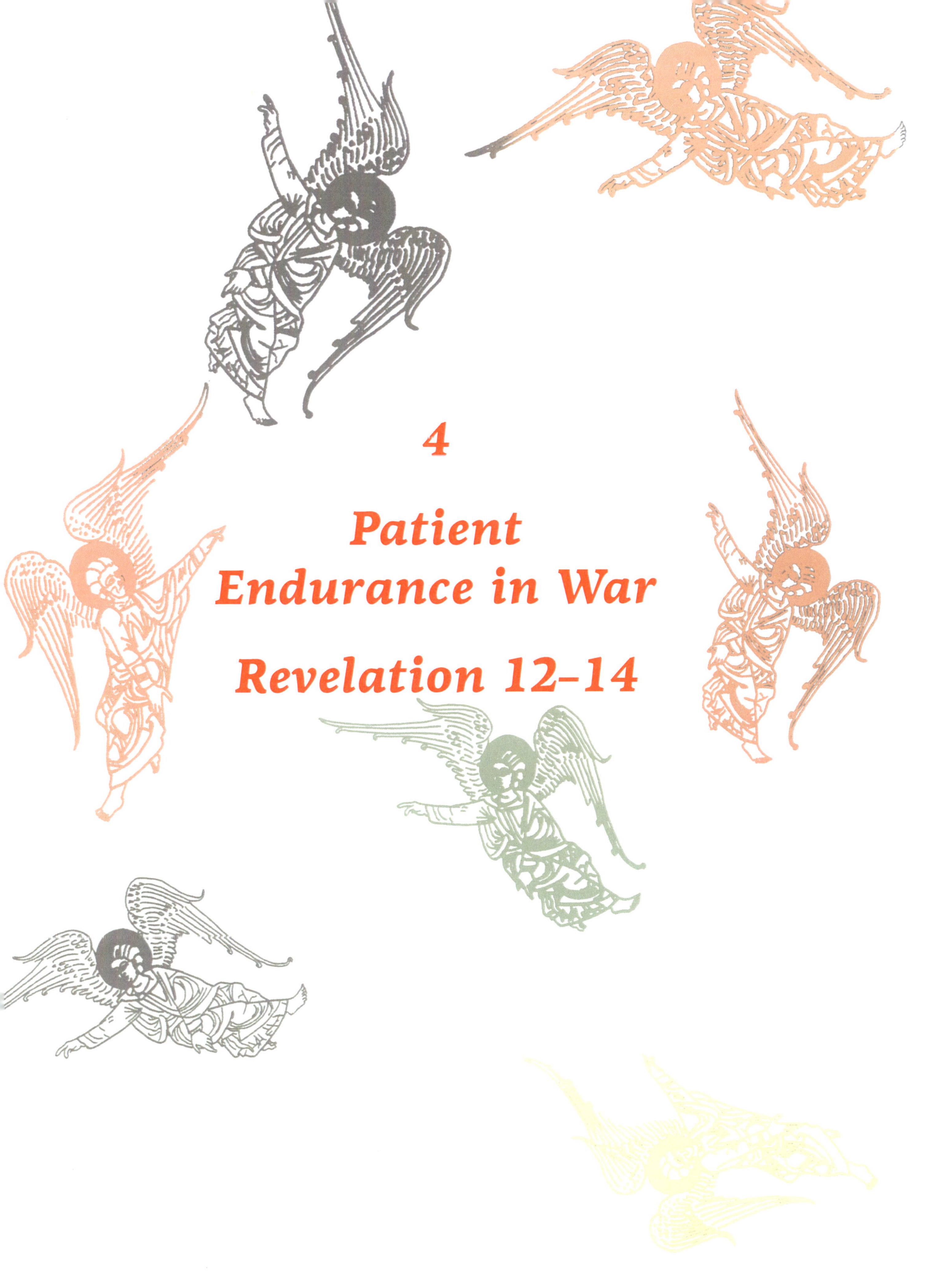

4

Patient Endurance in War

Revelation 12–14

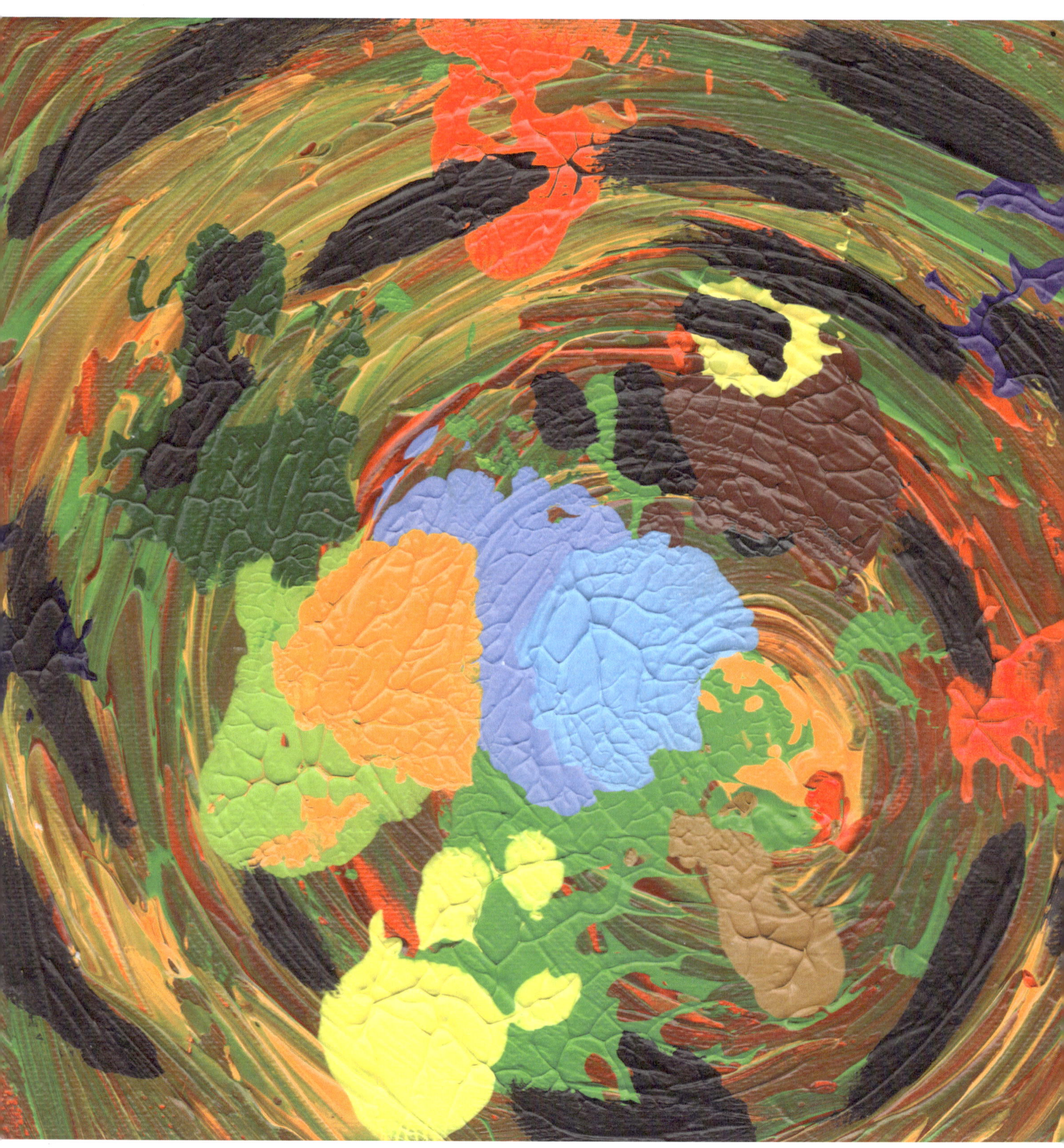

Interpreting Revelation
7'x7' acrylic on wood

Preface

I started this project reading and studying the Book of Revelation to satisfy my own interest in this spectacularly obscure book of the Bible. I did not have a publication in mind, but wanted to record my findings for my family, and particularly thought of my grandchildren, for times to come, perhaps, when I will not be around to talk to them about it. Once the idea of a publication floated up, my first question was, What sort of a book then? I certainly did not see the need for, or felt that I had any authority to write, yet another commentary on Revelation! There are some immense works by worthy scholars available today, even though not two are in complete agreement as to the meaning of the text! But when I had the idea of painting Revelation – it was after all given as visions at first – the format of this book immediately presented itself. It was never purely an art project for me, but always of seeking to understand the text by more directly interacting as an amateur artist with the Book of Revelation's visual references.

As I surveyed existing paintings on the Apocalypse, I came across the medieval "Illuminated" (illustrated) Apocalypses. A large number of them were created during distinct periods in the Middle Ages, often by "schools" of painters attached to a monastery. The sheer colour and beauty of their illustrations captivated me! As I read more about them, for I did not understand what I was seeing in the pictures, I soon realised that medieval iconography, with its set rules and "codes" for communicating meaning, represents a distinct visual "language"! That was exciting, and it helped me conceptualise my project. I also wondered whether it would be possible to trace the development of medieval theology simply by looking at the illustrations, but that proved not so simple. I came to understand that "reading" medieval manuscripts is a highly specialist field of study and had to rely heavily on the published wisdom of some excellent researchers who have done just that. I am thankful for their generosity and enthusiasm in sharing their findings and insights.

My interest is always primarily to inform my own understanding of the biblical text. But I also unashamedly love colour, so I highly recommend seeing the medieval manuscripts, for they are simply spectacularly beautiful!

In addition to the paintings, I also did a great deal of reading. In volumes 1–3, I list a selection of the books I have read. Here, however, I would like to highlight a few surprising reads:

Minear, Paul S. 1968. *I Saw a New Earth: An Introduction to the Visions of the Apocalypse*. Washington: Corpus Books. It contains a very convincing outline and some surprising and very inspirational essays. A most useful commentary for those who want to study Revelation for themselves. One of the very best for those who are starting off.

Bernier, Jonathan. 2022. *Rethinking the Dates of the New Testament: The Evidence for Early Composition*. Grand Rapids, Michigan: Baker Academic, a division of Baker Publishing Group. A convincing critique and update on A. T. Robinson's *Redating the New Testament*. It very helpfully argues for an early composition of the whole NT before AD 70.

Dawn, Marva J. 2001. *Powers, Weakness, and the Tabernacling of God*. Grand Rapids, Michigan: Eerdmans. This is one of the best books I have read on the subject of powers. After reading many more speculative accounts, it was a balm to my soul. Yes, they are real and dangerous, but Christ has and can conquer them through his and our weakness.

Didron, Adolphe Napoléon, and Margaret Stokes. 1851. *Christian Iconography: The History of Christian Art in the Middle Ages*. Translated by E. J. Millington. New York: F. Ungar Pub. Co. A wonderful treat to read this explaining the history of a large number of Christian symbols. And the development of the use of images of halos and the members of the Trinity is especially useful.

I thank God for health and strength to continue this project, and I thank each of the friends and acquaintances I have consulted along the way. Volumes 1 to 3 are now available as a single, combined edition. This Volume continues in the same format, starting at the end of Revelation 11 in the midst of a continuing series of visions following the blowing of the seventh trumpet.

Pieter Kwant, Manchester, UK, 2025

Medieval Illustrated Apocalypses

Canon 17 of the Fourth Synod of Toledo in 633 declared the Apocalypse to be a canonical book of the Bible, to be read in church from Easter to Pentecost. Illustrated copies of the Apocalypse may have been created as early as the fifth century and continued into the twelfth century, but they did not attract much attention until the twelfth to fifteenth centuries. A number of manuscript "families" have been identified. Local innovations were often introduced when the images were hand-copied, such as more contemporary costumes or architectural features. But once the printing press standardised output, such innovations stopped.

For interpreting medieval illustrations, I have relied on the following sources, listed in the bibliography: Peter Klein, John Williams, Nigel J. Morgan, Emmerson, Ian Short, Van der Meer, and others. I have compiled here a brief introduction for newcomers to the field. It is not a comprehensive introduction but concerns only the limited number I consulted. I am deeply indebted to the researchers who have studied them in depth and published their findings and insights so generously. Everything I know about medieval illustration, I learnt from them!

The first hurdle to cross when I started looking at these manuscripts, was how to locate copies of them. So, I include "fact boxes" here about the ones I consulted. Hopefully it will make it easier for readers who want to track them down for themselves.

I started with the *Rylands Beatus*, then moved on to the *Trinity Apocalypse*, followed by Dürer and the 1313 manuscript. I intended to restrict my references to these four, but as the world of illustrated Apocalypses opened up to me, I kept coming across more, and more different, manuscripts. It became difficult to keep track of the information as I had to do most of the research from home, relying on what is available online. My approach, to follow almost all the footnotes I came across, did help me eventually access most of them.

The next hurdle for me was deciphering the languages. Old Dutch, Old English and Old French are just as challenging to read as Latin, and I had to rely on the work done by the translators of these texts, such as Ian Short's translation of the *Trinity Apocalypse*. But I could find no translation of the Rylands manuscript and what I did find was not fit for purpose, which then led me to other Beatus manuscripts, especially ones with a larger number of scholarly studies published about them. The Silos manuscript became a personal favourite, despite the challenge of deciphering its Spanish!

It was an extremely joyful moment when I finally saw the original *Trinity Apocalypse* in Trinity Library in Cambridge, UK. I noticed details that were not visible in the electronic reproductions available on the internet. The "worked" gold surfaces, for example, and the ink colours and delicacy of the painted surfaces took my breath away and confirmed to me how truly magnificent this manuscript is!

What follows is not a beginner's history of medieval Apocalypse manuscripts, but simply a record of the ones I consulted. There are several "families" of manuscripts, where the same basic text was illustrated, and sometimes edited, for the particular context. Attempting a history, even a short one, would have made this a very long chapter, and histories are available for some of the works. My primary interest is in visual "commentary" on the whole of Revelation. But I urge readers to note the dates of the original manuscripts, as well as their physical sizes!

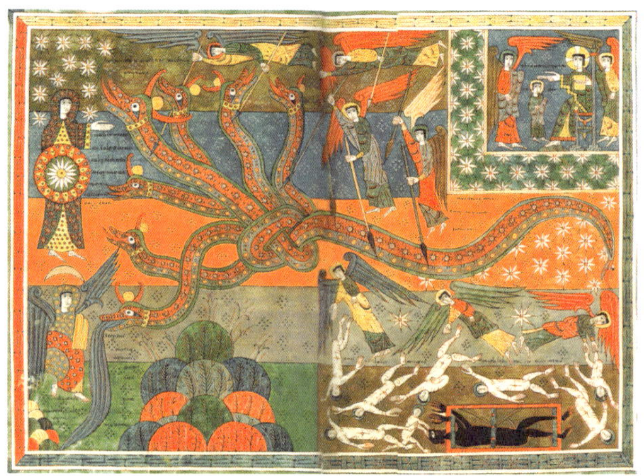

Beatus (AD776)

Where? No copy available
Origin? Liébana in Spain
Pages: More than 1000
Size: 454 x 326mm
Illustrations: 108 canonical images
Bible text: Old Latin, pre-Vulgate text identified with Africa

Beatus was a monk who lived in the Monastery of Santo Toribio de Liébana in Asturias in north-west Spain. Very little is known about his life. Neither the year of his birth nor of his death are recorded, but it is thought that he was born towards the middle of the eighth century and lived around 739–757.

Although the original Beatus manuscript is no longer available, a large family of copies exists, created over a period of several hundred years in different places. They are all referred to simply as "Beatus".

Today there are thirty-five Beatus manuscripts, of which around twenty-six are illuminated (or illustrated). They were produced over a period of three-and-a-half centuries, from the ninth to the thirteenth. It is the largest family of Apocalypse manuscripts dating from the Middle Ages.

Beatus was both editor and author of the Beatus. The triumph of a purified universal church under Christ is the underlying theme of his commentary text. Interestingly, the biblical text he used is not that of the Vulgate but an Old Latin text, from before the Vulgate and associated with Africa. Tyconius used the same text in his commentary. The commentary in the Beatus is a compilation of Beatus's own writing plus that of others, including Irenaeus (d. 203), Tyconius (d. 390), Jerome (d. 419), Augustine (d. 430), Aspringius (d. 540) and Isidore (d. 636). Many Church Fathers are also referenced. Tyconius was clearly the most important source, so much so that the Beatus has been used to reconstruct Tyconius's original, of which no complete copy survived.

The Beatus contains many introductions and tributes, but the main body is divided into sixty-eight sections of approximately twelve biblical verses each, known as "Storiae" (64), which present the text from 1:1 to 22:21. Three small sections are treated differently. The division into Storiae may have been introduced when the decision was made to illustrate the text. Each Storia is followed by a series of exegetical passages that interpret the text allegorically and analogically. In *Inside the Rainbow* I have adopted a similar structure, dividing the text into smaller sections according to how I can feasibly represent that text section with an image to remind me of the biblical text and recall it in prayer.

It was the 108 canonical images that accompany the Beatus that made it famous. The illustrators of Beatus generally followed the biblical narrative rather than its interpretation, with a few exceptions. Sixty-eight illustrations are based on the narrative according to the Storiae structure; seven are based on the text of the commentary rather than the biblical text; there are eight prefatory or introductory miniatures of the Evangelists and their Gospels; fourteen illustrations are based on the genealogy of Christ; and eleven are based on Daniel. The illustrations most likely accompanied the earliest manuscript, as they are fully integrated with the text. Most historians believe these illustrations were copied from earlier, pre-Beatus, manuscripts. Some suggest that Tyconius's commentary may have been illustrated, and that it provided the inspiration for Beatus. However, it is also possible that it all started in Liébana.

The illustration style in Beatus is called "Mozarabic" (or "Arabicised"), a term that refers to the culture and language of Christians in the Iberian Peninsula under Arab occupation from the early eighth until about the fourteenth century, as well as those whose lives were shaped there before they migrated north. Although the Beatus commentaries and other Mozarabic Christian manuscripts have been suggested as examples of the influence of Islamic style, it is not possible to clearly document their debt to Islamic painting in the fundamental areas of format and colour, or in the design of figures and ornamentation.

Interesting fact 1: In the 800s, people had a heightened expectation of Christ's imminent return.
Interesting fact 2: There is some debate as to when St Jerome's commentary on the biblical book of Daniel was added to some Beatus manuscripts (while the biblical text in the Beatus is pre-Vulgate).
Fun fact: 19 February (my own birthday) is the feast day of St Beatus!

Intended primary readers: Monks, using it for devotional reading; and later lay readers too, but secondary.

The Beatus is "supra-historical": it applies the biblical text to all situations. It elucidates Revelation in ecclesiological terms, emphasising the relentless struggle between the forces of Christ and the antiChrist, experienced, for example, between true and false churches. Furthermore, Beatus was the first to depict the antiChrist as a human being (150v–151r, Morgan Beatus).

The Morgan Beatus (AD945)

Where? New York, USA: The Morgan Library & Museum; MS 644
Origin? San Salvador de Tábara, in Spain
Pages: 300
Size: 387 x 285mm
Illustrations: 110 miniatures
Bible text: Latin

In the mid-tenth century, a Spanish monk and painter named Maius was commissioned by the abbot of the Leonese Monastery of St Michael to create a copy of the Beatus commentary. This is now the earliest Beatus manuscript available.

Materials and quality: The 300 leaves of the manuscript were made of high-quality parchment that is thick and uniformly coloured. The margins are wide and the script and illuminations are well preserved except for several leaves that have been damaged by damp or fire. The colours are remarkably well preserved and vibrant.

An interesting fact: Maius wrote as follows about the purpose of his illustrations: "I have painted this series of pictures for the wonderful words of its stories so that the wise may fear the coming of the future judgement of the end of the world."

In other words, Maius's aim was for the pictorial depictions to make the verbal accounts of the Storiae more immediate. There would probably have been specific "rules" for the illustrations to be considered canonical, which was necessary for the commentary to be acceptable for reading in monasteries. Such rules would reflect the official church interpretation of the text at the time, and would not have allowed for an explicit, individual exegesis.

The Silos Beatus (AD1109)

Where: London, British Library; MS Add. 11695
Origen: The Benedictine monastery of Santo Domingo de Silos in Spain
Pages: 280 folios
Size: 380 x 240mm
Illustrations: 106 miniatures; or 53 full-page miniatures, some of which extend onto the facing page, as well as another 77 smaller images
Bible text: Latin

The Silos contains information about some of its creators, including two scribes named Dominicus and Munnius, as well as an illuminator named Prior Petrus. Information of its illustrations often provide different numbers, based on which illustrations are included: miniatures (distinct independent paintings illustrating the text); decorated initials; and/or marginalia (playful, small drawings in the manuscript margins). Illustration descriptions for the Silos is particularly complex because its artistic style blends the Mozarabic from earlier Beatus manuscripts with the newer Romanesque.

The text contains a fragment of an antiphon in addition to the commentary of Beatus, extracts from the Etymologies by Isidore of Seville, the commentary by St Jerome on the biblical Book of Daniel, and various other texts, some which are attributed to St Jerome, St Gregory the Great and St Augustine.

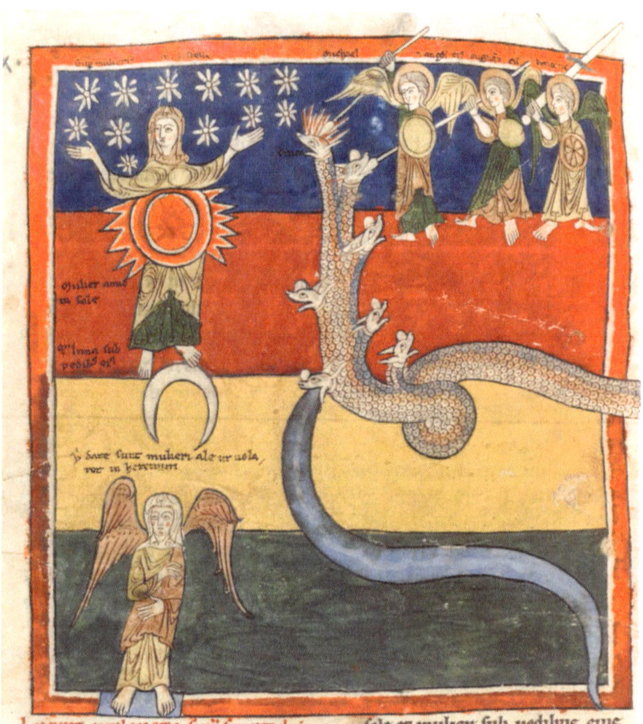

Fun fact: In addition to the main Beatus texts, this manuscript contains music for the Divine Office liturgy.

The Silos Codex ("Codex" refers to the shape of the manuscript that is bound as a book, but hand-written, and not a scroll) is one of the most important surviving Beatus manuscripts thanks to its large format, its numerous and vivid illustrations, and its excellent state of preservation.

The Rylands Beatus (AD1175)

Where? Manchester, UK: John Rylands Library; MS Lat. 8
Origin? The Monastery of San Pedro de Cardeña in Castrello de Val in Spain
Pages: 510
Size: 454mm x 326mm
Illustrations: 123 miniatures
Text: Latin, Romanesque

I will never forget how surprised I was by the size of the MS facsimile when I handled it for the first time. It was huge and magnificent!

Important note: One of the original scenes depicts Noah's Ark as a building filled with pairs of animals, framed by what appears to be small square windows. With this, the illuminator emphasised the redemptive role of the revelation, and the theme of spiritual warfare by depicting scenes of war and siege alongside fighting animals, for example the full-page miniature depicting a bird killing a serpent.

Other Medieval Apocalypse Manuscripts or Families of Manuscripts

The Trier Apocalypse (AD800)

Where? Trier, Germany: Stadtbibliothek; MS 31
Origin? Tours in France
Pages: 75 folios
Size: 262 x 216mm
Illustrations: 74, presenting 150 individual narrative episodes
Bible text: Latin Vulgate

There is no commentary in the Trier, only the biblical text. The Trier shows no interest in historical development, focusing instead on the timeless ecclesiological allegory of the battle between good and evil, following the standard exegetical approach that distinguishes between true and false churches: Ecclesia versus Synagogue; New Jerusalem versus Babylon.

Unlike most manuscripts, the Trier includes a visual commentary on the content of the seven churches.

Although the Trier is often described as a literal illustration of Scripture, it is selective in what it represents, sometimes ignoring discursive details and sometimes adding figural features that are unrelated to the text.

Materials: Ink and pen, with a little pale watercolour. Everything looks a bit rushed.

Design: The text is divided into sixty-one sections, but the relationship between the text and the illustrations is unclear. Folios 1–20 have illustrations on the verso, then the recto. According to R. K. Emmerson, the Trier establishes a coherent relationship between the biblical text and its visual representation.

Fun fact: John is the artist's favourite "filler" and appears over seventy times. On folio 51r, the small figure represents the false prophet, who has a square, uncoloured nimbus instead of a golden one. This is an effective visual way of distinguishing between good and bad prophets.

Interesting fact: Certain stylistic features suggest that the images were copied from an earlier, sixth-century, manuscript; and that those illustrations, in turn, may have been based on an illustrated edition of Tyconius's now-lost commentary on Revelation.

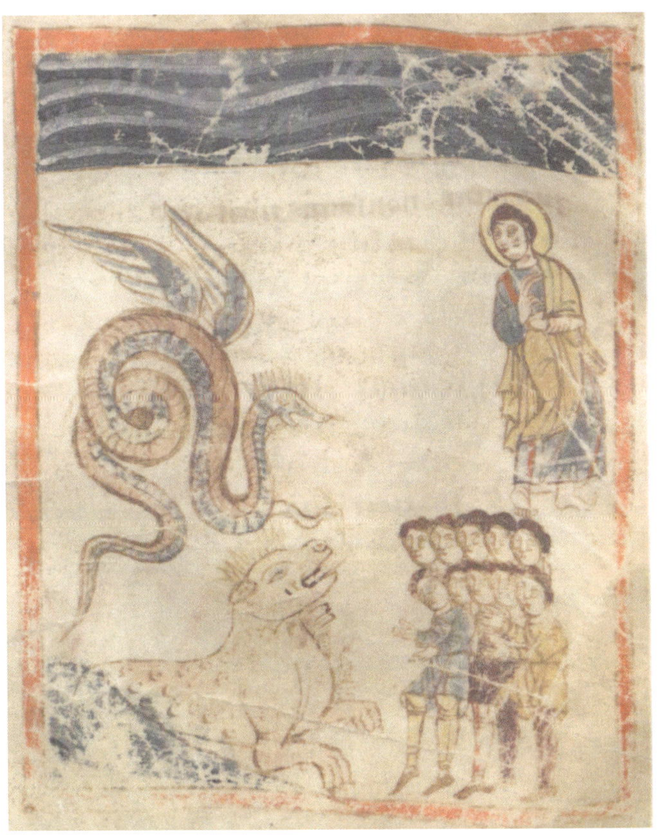

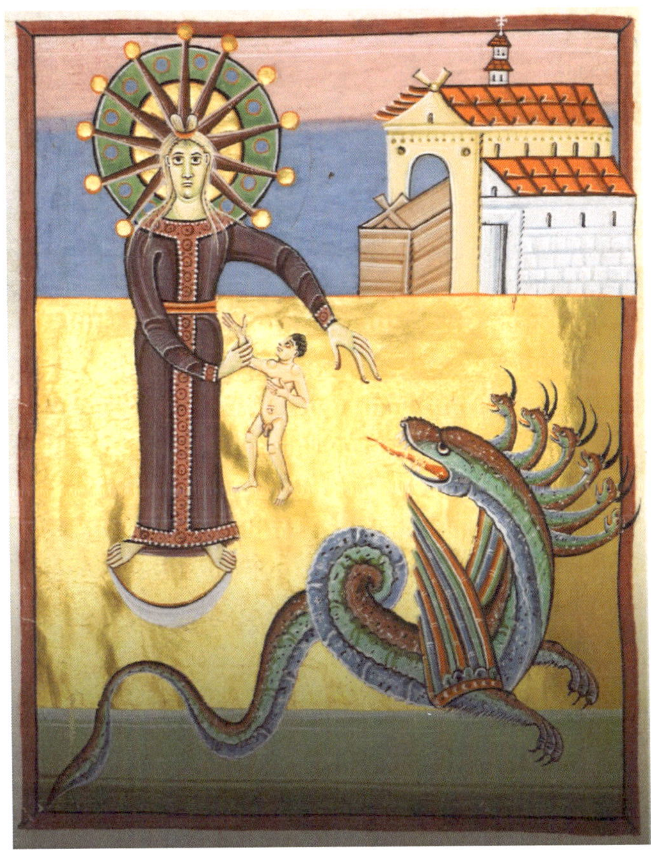

The Bamberg Apocalypse (AD1000)

Where? Bamberg, Germany: Staatsbibliothek; Msc.Bibl.140
Origin? The scriptorium of Reichenau Abbey, Reichenau, Germany (formerly part of the Holy Roman Empire)
Pages: 106 folios
Size: 295 x 205mm
Illustrations: 57 gilded miniatures and over 100 gilded initials
Bible text: Latin (Vulgate?)
Online: https://artsandculture.google.com/exhibit/the-bamberg apocalypse/VwKiP_Fswg0iLw

This Apocalypse was commissioned by Emperor Otto III at the turn of the first millennium. The Bamberg Apocalypse is a masterpiece of Ottonian book illumination.

The manuscript contains the Latin text of the biblical Book of Revelation, followed by a Gospel lectionary with readings for the major church feasts from Nativity to Pentecost. Its scope is wide, including Christ, the church, and the end times. Van der Meer is full of praise for this manuscript:

"The Trier is a document; the Bamberg is a great work of art!" He refers to the artist of the Bamberg manuscript as "an unconscious surrealist".

The Bamberg illustrations are remarkable for their jewel-toned colours, gilded backgrounds, and intensity of gesture and movement. In addition to vivid illustrations of events from the life of Christ and the end of the world, the two parts of this lavish book are divided by Otto's portrait (folio 59v–60r). In the first part, the Apocalypse is depicted in fifty miniatures; the Gospel lectionary in the second part contains illustrations too.

Fun fact: The Bamberg Apocalypse contains a remarkable portrait of the young Otto III being crowned by Saints Peter and Paul, while personifications of the Empire look on adoringly.

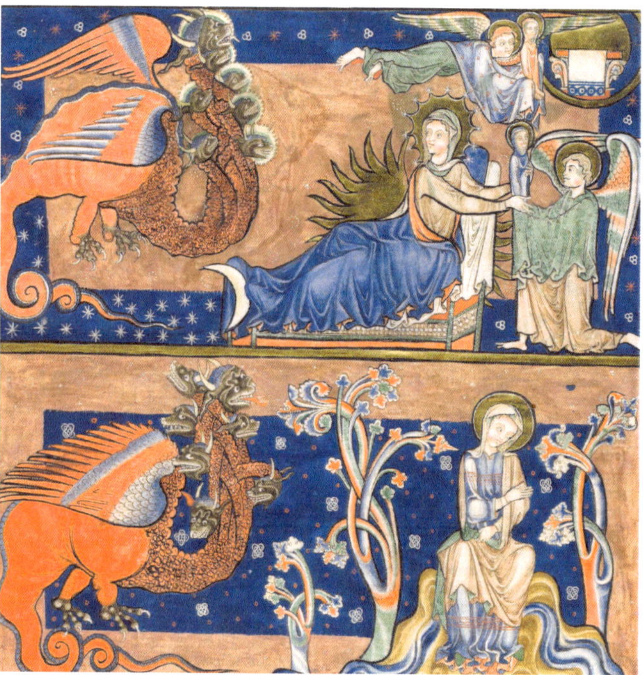

The Trinity Apocalypse (AD1260)

Where? Cambridge, UK: The Library of Trinity College; MS. R16.2
Origin? Possibly North France, North Spain or England
Pages: 32 folios
Size: 430mm x 304mm
Illustrations: 75
Bible text: Anglo-Norman biblical text, with Berengaudus commentary excerpts
Online: Msscat.trin.cam.ac.uk/Manuscript/R.16.2/UV#?c=0&m=0&s=0&cv=0&r=0&xywh=-2802%2C-537%2C12612%2C10707

The Trinity Apocalypse is notable because it contains both the biblical text and extracts from Berengaudus's commentary in the vernacular. Hand-written in Gothic Textualis by a scribe, the text is mostly set out in two columns, except when the commentary on a particular part of the text is particularly long. It then is written in long lines. Blue or red initials with flourishes introduce each section of the text, and the biblical sections are numbered in red and blue Roman numerals. The splendour of the decoration makes this a book fit for a queen!

An important fact is that three brief but significant passages in the commentary remind us, albeit indirectly, that the primary function of the book in the mid-thirteenth century was to bring the Scriptures in both written and pictorial form to a wider audience.

Berengaudus divides Revelation into seven visions, interpreting them both historically and prophetically. The seven horns of the Lamb allude to the seven ages of world history. These ages represent seven categories of God's elect: those living before Noah's flood; those under the Law; the prophets; Jews who believe in Christ; Gentiles who believe in Christ; and finally, those born in the last days who will fight the antiChrist. The silence in Revelation 8:1 represents the Pax Romana at the time of Christ's birth.

The Getty Apocalypse (AD1260)

Where? Paul Getty Museum, Los Angeles, USA: J. Paul Getty Museum; Ludwig III1 (Getty or Dyson Perrins Apocalypse) 83.MC.72
Origin? There is no convincing evidence where this manuscript originated
Pages: 42 folios (incomplete)
Size: 330mm x 241mm
Illustrations: 92
Bible text: Latin Vulgate, with selections of Berengaudus's commentary
Materials: Tempera paints, gold leaf, coloured washes, and ink
Design: Each Image with biblical text and commentary on the same folio
Fun fact: John often appears out of the frame, looking in.

For me, it is one of the most beautiful depictions of the Apocalypse. The illustrations communicate clearly, and I love the visual interactions with John. I also like the choice of imagery. With the whole text in English has made this manuscript so much more accessible for me than many of the others.

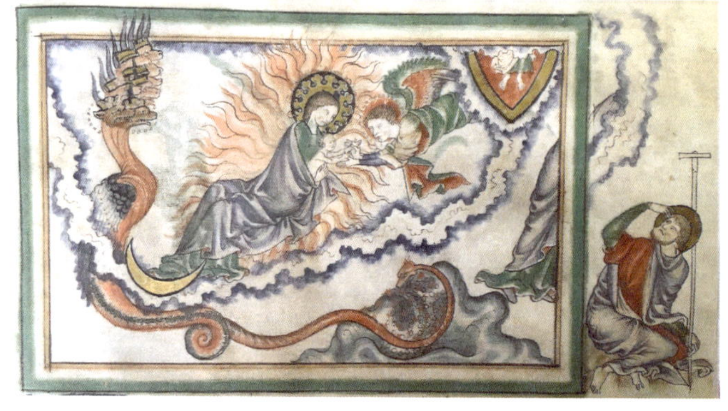

The Gulbenkian Apocalypse (AD1275)

Where? Lisbon, Museu Calouste Gulbenkian, L.A. 139
Origin? England
Pages: 76 folios (152p)
Size: 273mm x 216mm
Illustrations: 153
Bible text: Latin Vulgate and Selections of the Berengaudus's commentary

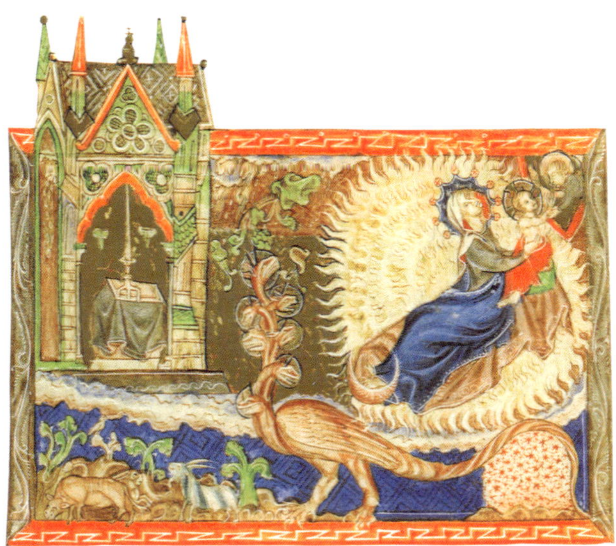

Each folio contains a miniature, a section of bible text, and a section of commentary by Berengaudus. The miniature is placed at the top of the page and all illustrations are surrounded by a rectangular frame intended to enhance rather than separate the illustration. Indeed, figures and architectural structures often extend beyond the frames.

The illustrations feature densely populated imagery, enhanced by burnished gold and vibrant colours such as red, blue and green. The artist demonstrates great skill in the use of colour and gold, creating miniatures that are highly evocative and representative of the text and glosses. One of the most famous illustrations is the miniature on folio 1r, which depicts St John on the island of Patmos receiving a message from Christ via an angel.

Note: To study old manuscripts, it helps to be familiar with printing and binding terminology. Each folded sheet is a bifolium, which is two folios (leaves). And the whole stack of sheets is called a "gathering". Depending on the number of sheets you have used, there will be either 8 or 10 folios. When these leaves are written and bound, the collection is called a "quire".

The 1313 Apocalypse (AD1313)

Where? Paris, France: Bibliothèque nationale de France; Fr. 13096
Origin? France
Pages: 167 folios (344 pages)
Size: 237 x 164mm
Illustrations: 162
Text: French bible text plus commentary

This manuscript is a unique creation, signed and dated in 1313 by its illuminator, Colin Chadewe. It contains one of the most extensive cycles of illustrations, characterised by their richness and eccentric iconography. These were designed exclusively to meet the demands of the patron.

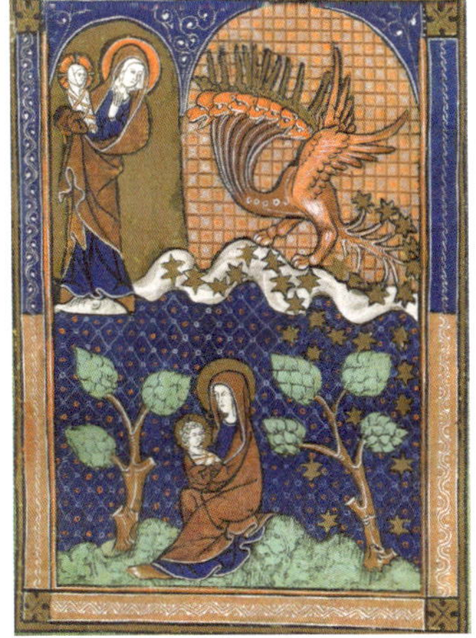

Each project has a manuscript organiser who lays it out at the patron's request and according to their instructions. In the 1313 they had 21 quires to work with, and there is plenty of evidence of the huge challenges they faced in fitting text and image together.

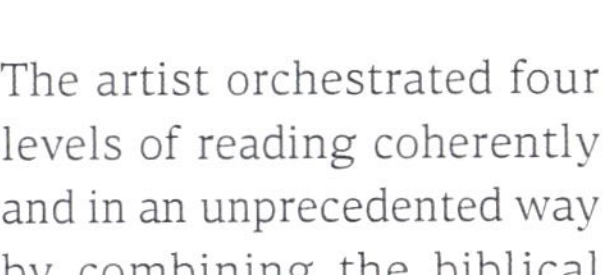

The artist orchestrated four levels of reading coherently and in an unprecedented way by combining the biblical text of the Apocalypse with traditional iconographic models and various commentaries, as well as his own interpretation of the texts. This allows us to perceive a whole new set of meanings in the work.

The design: This Apocalypse is exceptional because it is a rare example of a French manuscript from the early fourteenth century that shows few traces of the Parisian style. It stands out for its extraordinary quality and uniqueness, both textually and iconographically. It appears to be an unusual adaptation of various sources including the Liber Floridus, the Beatus tradition and the well-established Gothic English Apocalypse tradition.

History: The 1313 is a very representative example of its time, "a period when laymen enamoured of perfection and tales of chivalry were delighted to find epic inspiration in the illustrations of Scripture" (Gousset).

The Apocalypse of Val-Dieu (AD1330)

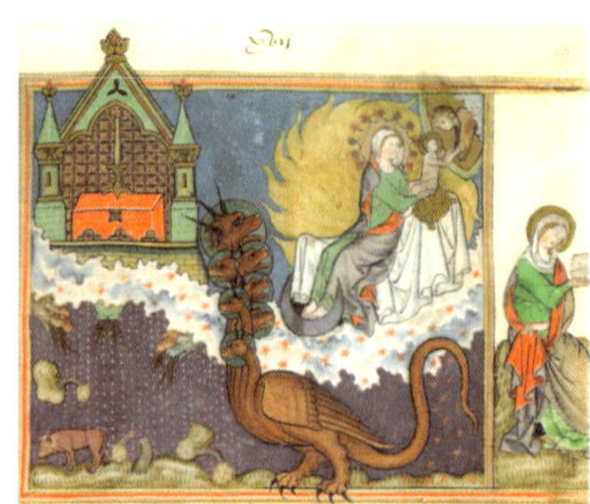

Where? London: British Library; Add. MS. 17333
Origin: Lorraine, Normandy
Pages: 54 folios (108 pages)
Size: 325 x 225mm
Illustrations: 83
Bible text: French plus Latin Vulgate (1320-30), transition period from Old to Middle French. No commentary
Design: Based on the Metz and Lambeth Apocalypses; 53 illustrations are almost identical and 22 are from an extended Metz. There are also 4 new scenes.

In Normandy, the preferred format was pictures and text. Miniatures were placed at the top with the text below. This was usually the Latin text of the Bible plus some commentary, most often extracts from Berengaudus, but not here.

Important fact: Special, superior painting quality and stunning imagery worked by brilliant colourists in, for example, lavender, plum, and dark green.

This is one of the later Apocalypses that I came across, and I have grown to like its imagery very much. Although the colour palette is darker than I prefer, it is vibrant and the imagery, innovative. The following video by the publisher Moleiro provides an insight into the process of creating modern facsimiles of this beautiful and inspiring manuscript: https://www.youtube.com/playlist?list=PLGapGlViYRH3Tk38FobjsF8cOp1pdoo87

Picture Book of the Life of St John and the Apocalypse (Tongerlo) (AD1400)

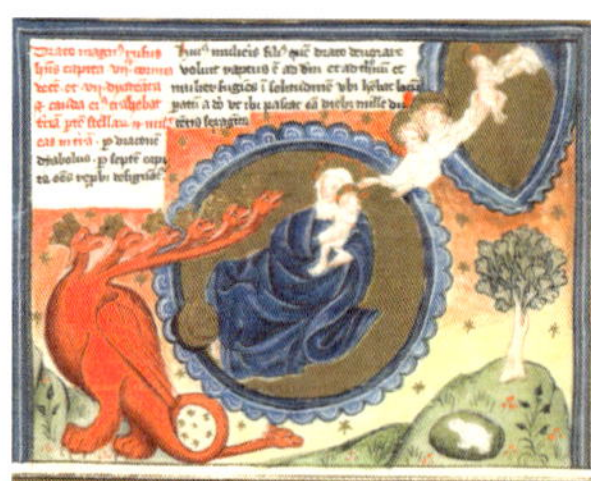

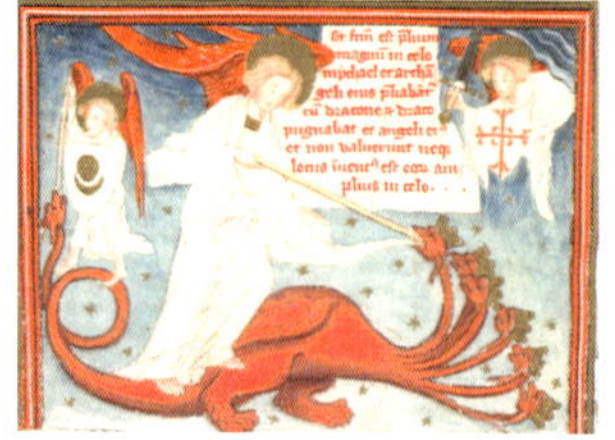

Where? London, UK: British Library; Add Ms 38121
Origin? Belgium, Brabant
Pages: 47 folios (94 pages)
Size: 335 x 230mm
Illustrations: 94 images
Text: Anglo-French Bible text and Berengaudus comments inside the illumination
Design: Two images per page, all painted on the back of the pages leaving the front open for the biblical text. The Bible text is randomly placed next to the image on the verso as the text and illuminations do not correspond. Therefore, the text must be read independently of the illuminations, which contain their own texts.

An important fact: There is biblical and commentary text (Berengaudus) within the pictures, giving them a contemporary cartoon or graphic novel feel. This manuscript belongs to the picture book group.

During this period, many Apocalypse cycles included an introduction to the life of John. In this manuscript, it appears on four pages at the beginning and three at the end. The manuscript also contains five scenes depicting the life of the antiChrist, who is portrayed as a man based on extra-biblical material and medieval antiChrist legends.

Apocalipsis in Dietsche /Flemish Apocalypse (AD1410)

Where? Paris, France: Bibliothèque nationale de France; néerlandais 3
Origin? Flanders
Pages: 23 folios (46 pages)
Size: 338 x 248mm
Illustrations: 23 full page images
Text: Flemish Bible text
Design: Bible text on versos, with all illustrations on rectos. The illustrations are full narrative paintings of the text.

Fun fact: The illustrator made a big mistake when painting the miniature for Revelation 16. Instead of painting it on the recto of the folio, with Revelation 17 on its verso, he inadvertently painted it on the recto of folio 20. Consequently, the miniature illustrating Revelation 17 is now opposite the text of Revelation 20!

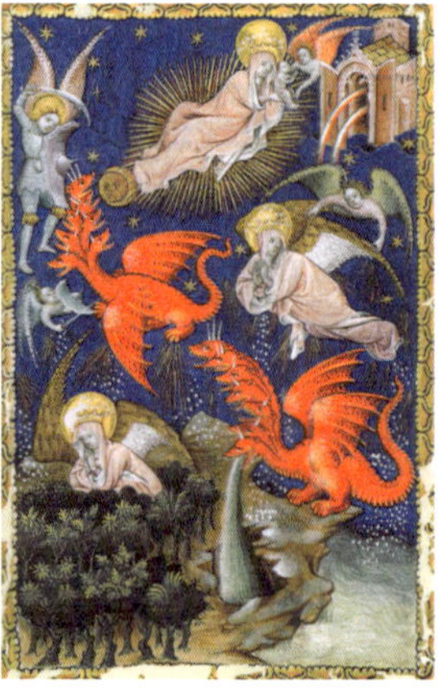

The Flemish Apocalypse is not only a late example of the Anglo-Norman tradition, but also a monument of pre-Eyckian realism. It is one of my favourite Apocalypses. I love the narrative style, which means you can't stop looking at the illustrations. There is always more to see. The tonal differences are sometimes so minimal that you have to look very closely to see everything, which mimics the text that works in a similar way. This manuscript achieves in twenty-three pictures what others can only achieve in over ninety!

Blockbook (AD1430)

Where? London, UK: The British Museum, and for sale online at Abe Books
Origin? The Low Countries (Leuven in Belgium and Utrecht in the Netherlands)
Pages: 25 folios (50 pages)
Size: 300 x 216mm
Illustrations: 100
Text: Inside the illustrations in Old Dutch
Design: 2 illustrations to a page, fully integrated with the text

Fun fact: In some cases, the illustrations were hand-painted after the books were printed!

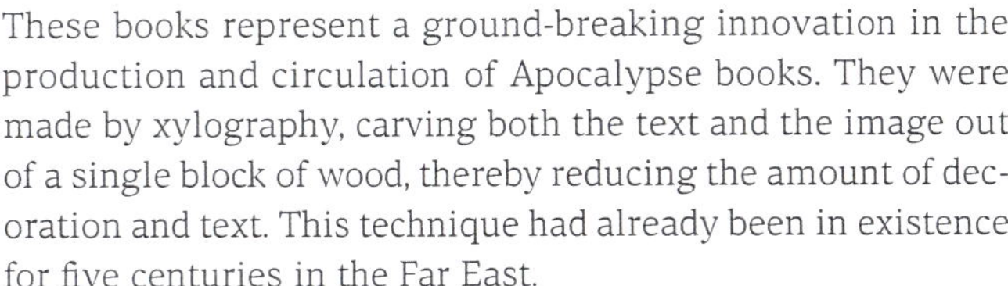

These books represent a ground-breaking innovation in the production and circulation of Apocalypse books. They were made by xylography, carving both the text and the image out of a single block of wood, thereby reducing the amount of decoration and text. This technique had already been in existence for five centuries in the Far East.

The edition I used was published by Prestel Verlag in 1961 and is called: "Die Urausgabe der Holländischen Apokalypse und Biblia Pauperum". It made an illustrated Apocalypse accessible to a wider readership.

Dürer's Apocalypse: Apocalypsis cum figuris (AD1498)

Where? It is best to access the images on the internet
Origin? Germany, Nuremberg
Pages: 15 pages
Size: 390 x 280mm
Illustrations: 15 large woodcuts, of exquisite quality that have certainly stood the test of time
Text: No text

Interesting fact: This was the first time an artist designed and published a book under his own name. The project was a huge commercial success.

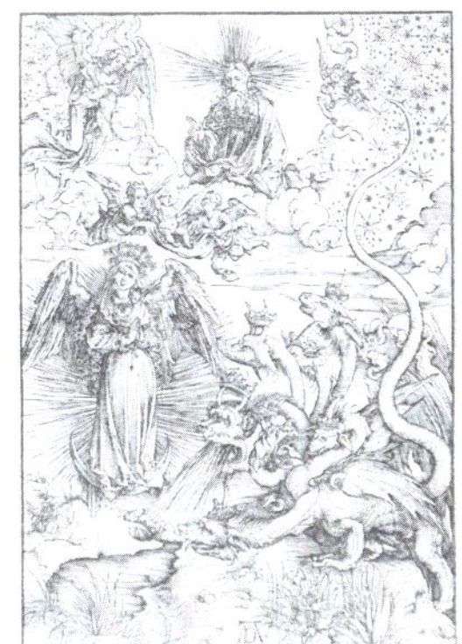

History: Some of these images, especially the Four Horsemen, have become iconic over the centuries and are still used in both religious and secular contexts. I have used Dürer's prints extensively in my books. This was a Reformation project.

Although Dürer was sympathetic to Luther's Protestant cause, he never left the Catholic Church, hoping rather to reform it from within. His project was the first attempt to print and distribute images of the Apocalypse individually, and without added text, to communicate biblical meaning. In that, they represent "pure" visual exegesis.

Dürer's project launched European religious publishing as a commercially viable enterprise to distribute Bible knowledge in large quantities and widely beyond the monasteries.

"Apocalypse" in Luther's Bible, ill. Cranach (AD1534)

Where? A facsimile edition in 2 volumes has been published by Taschen
Origin? Germany
Pages: 36, for the Book of Revelation
Size: 244 x 154mm
Illustrations: 26 woodcuts, out of total of 117 in the complete Bible
Text: German, Luther's translation
Design: Illustration within the text usually comes at the top of a page

Fun facts: The artist, Lucas Cranach, was clearly inspired by Dürer. *The Luther Bible* is now available in full colour! It sold over 100,000 copies in Luther's time – a first "bestseller"! Those copies were all individually hand-coloured!

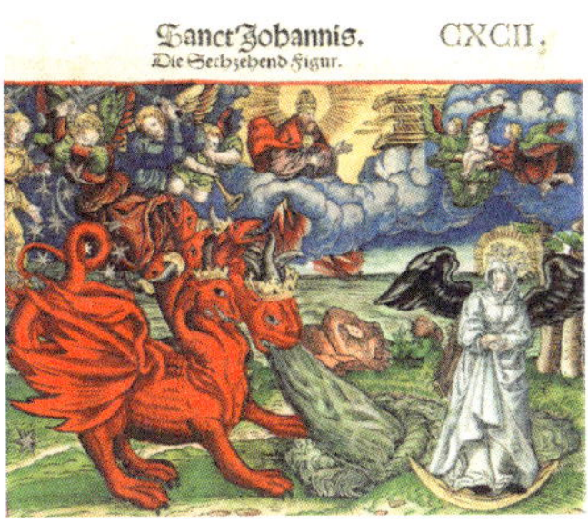

Duvet's Apocalypse (AD1561)

Where? Available online through Abe Books
Origin? Langres, France, though Jean Duvet lived and worked mainly in Geneva in Switzerland
Pages: 30
Size: 280 x 204mm
Illustrations: 23 engravings
Text: No text
Design: Naive Expressionism or Mannerism

Fun fact: Duvet refused to distinguish between the realms of heaven and earth. The natural and supernatural appear locked together in a struggle, but it is difficult to discern the details.

Heavily influenced by Dürer, Duvet's work is less refined and more emotional and expressionist. I find the darkness of the woodcuts rather depressing.

A Great Sign, a Woman

The sound of the seventh trumpet still rings in John's ears. And the noise in the heavenly temple and the sight of the ark of the covenant still lingers as a new great sign appears in heaven: a woman, crying out in labour, which is how I painted her, with the help of Feibush. In the medieval depiction, for example in the Getty image below, she is shown at peace and tranquil, which to our scientific minds appears strange in the context.

12: [1]A great portent appeared in heaven: a woman clothed with the sun, with the moon under her feet, and on her head a crown of twelve stars. [2]She was pregnant and was crying out in birth pangs, in the agony of giving birth.

Who is this woman? Unlike the dragon that appears later on, the woman is not given a name. I wonder if this was intentional. There are multiple suggestions: Mary; or Eve; the ethnic descendants of Jacob; the people of God; the faithful community of Zion; the NT people of God; the church and so on. Personally, I think Eve is a good choice to start with when reading this story in light of the next one, and considering the cosmic scope of the whole. Eve's opponent is the ancient serpent. Her portrayal, clothed with the sun and having the moon under her feet while wearing a crown of twelve stars, is reminiscent of Joseph's dream in Genesis. The heavenly bodies show her glory. As mother of all the living, she encompasses all "life-givers", including Mary as well as all God's holy people. I find no need to introduce pagan mythology to explain what is shown, in the way many commentators do. In my painting, I express the cosmic nature of this vision by including real galaxies in the background.

Who is the child? A number of suggestions have been made. The ancients saw this child as the church. Some contemporary scholars agree with that interpretation, but most agree that this child refers to Jesus, and I also find that the most likely and simplest interpretation.

In most illuminated manuscripts, the vision of the heavenly ark is depicted at the beginning of Revelation 12, with the visions of the ark and of the woman often appearing in the same illustration.

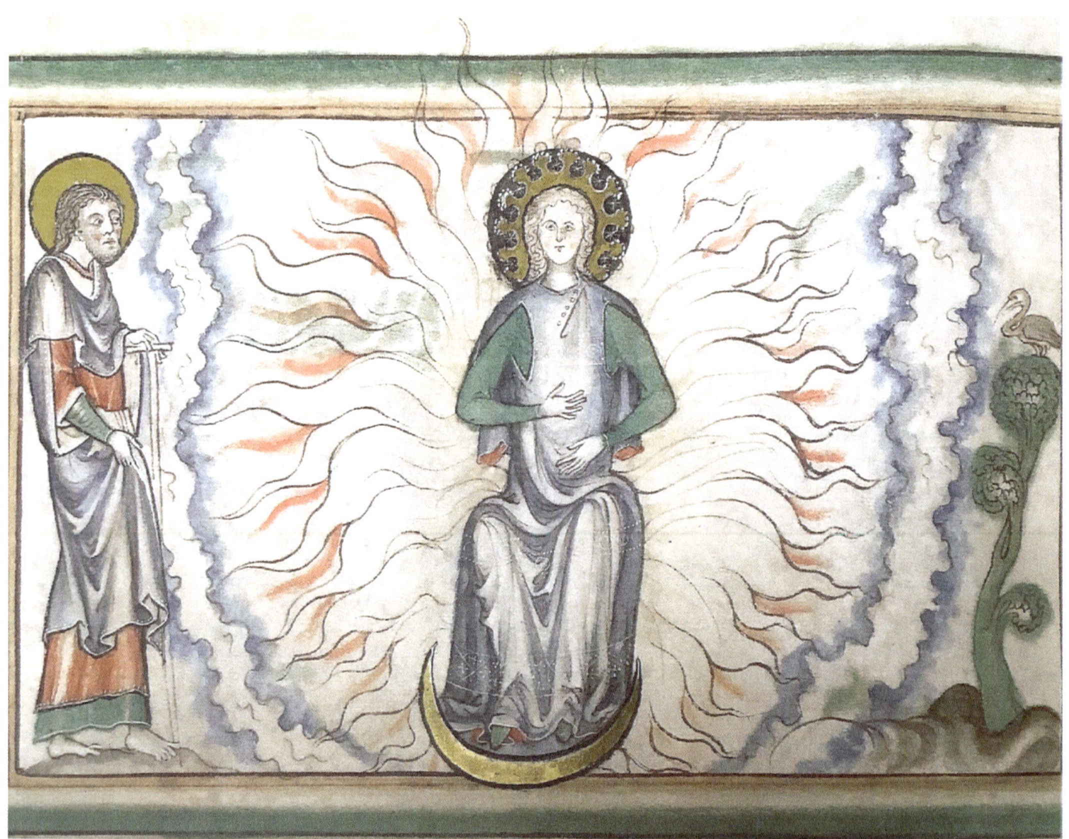

I have kept them separate, for I feel that the ark belongs to both Revelation 11, which it closes, and Revelation 12, where it is the opening sign in the next series of portents.

John calls this vision of the woman "a great sign". The reason for its greatness will become clear in what follows. As I see it, the woman signifies what has been true and will be true for God's people in all places and times: that in His Kingdom their experience of (temporary) agony goes hand in hand with (eventual) great glory. And this will be developed as we read on.

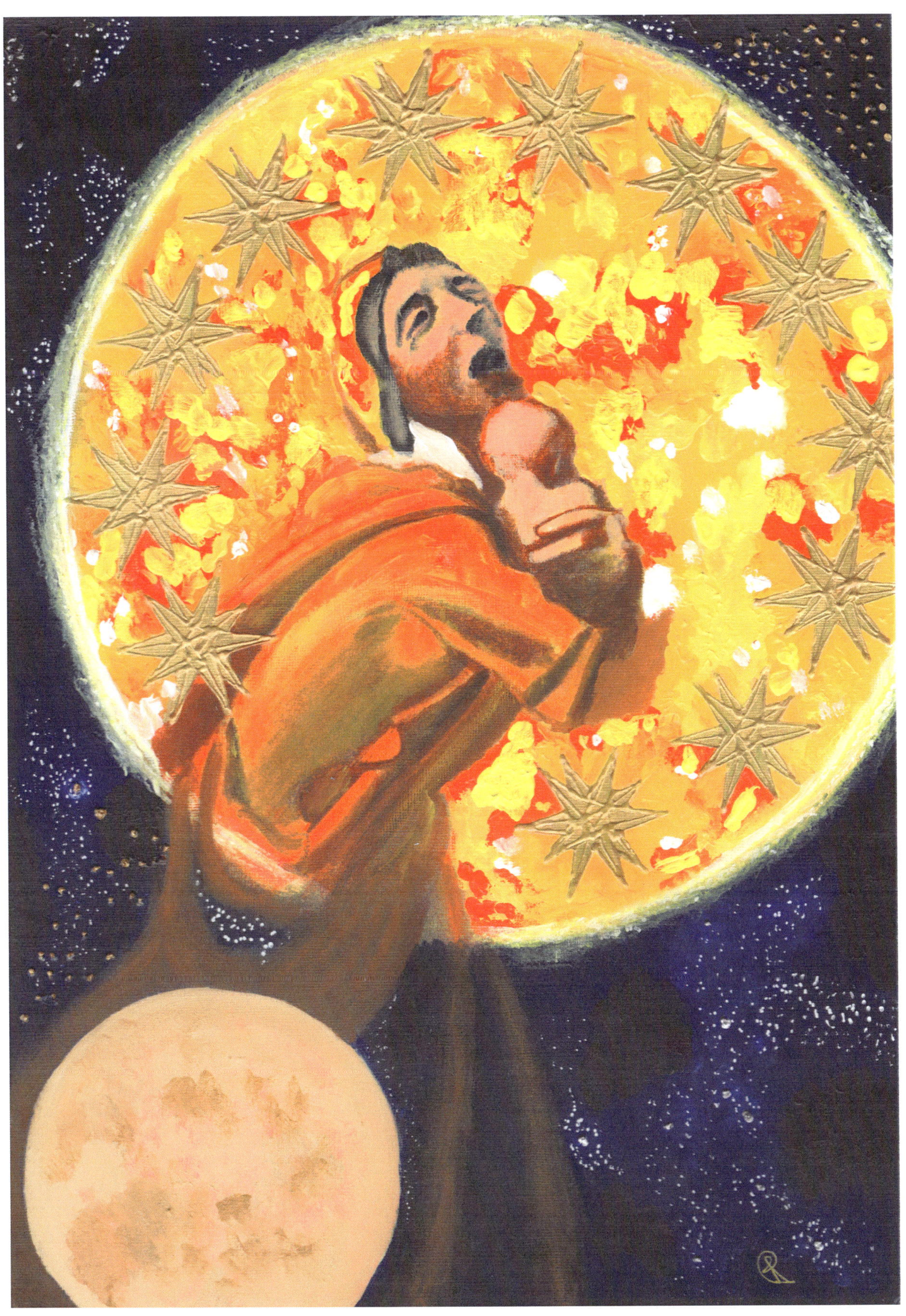

Another Sign, a Great Serpent

Following the vision of the woman, another portent follows. The fact that "heaven" can also mean "sky" has led some commentators to suggest that the dragon should be interpreted as the constellation Draco. But John is not describing an experience of looking at the sky at night (as noted in Rev 11). This sign introduces John to the dragon. Though he has encountered the dragon in the letters to the churches and in the seals and trumpets, John has never yet seen him. Now he sees the dragon. The opening of the scroll reveals all!

In my painting, the presence of the dragon darkens part of the sky and extends to the earth. I have painted stars to depict the dragon removing a third of them. John can see what is normally unseen: the spiritual world of angels, powers, authorities and demons, which exists in what can be called the "in-between" world.

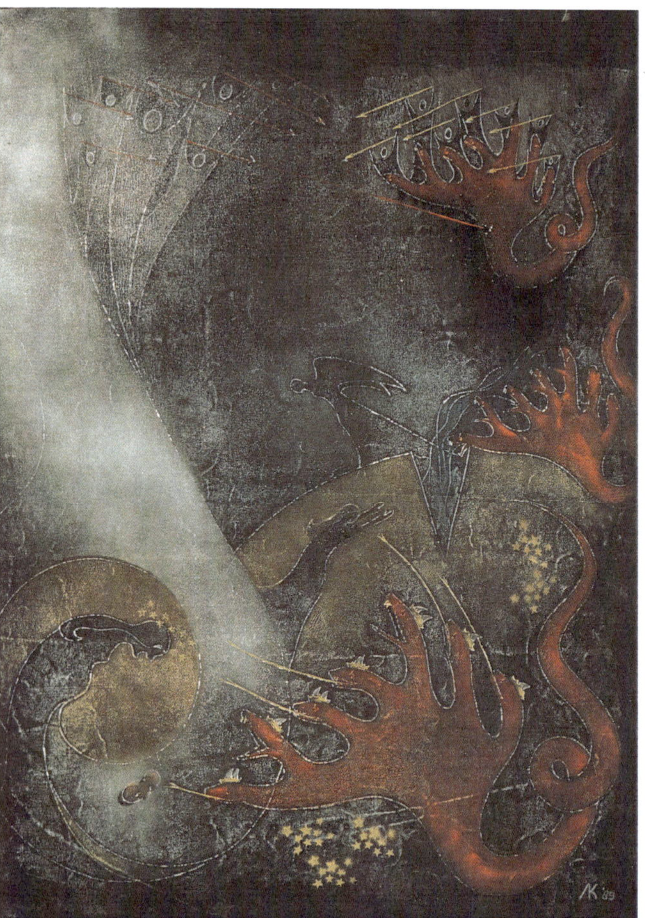

12: [3]Then another portent appeared in heaven: a great red dragon, with seven heads and ten horns, and seven diadems on his heads. [4]His tail swept down a third of the stars of heaven and threw them to the earth ...

[9]that ancient serpent, who is called the devil and Satan, the deceiver of the whole world.

So, what characterises this dragon? First, the dragon is a beast, an authority not a human being. Secondly, he has seven heads, a reminder that he represents "complete" or total evil. His ten horns show his terrible power. In my painting I placed his horns on his tail because those horns affect a third of the stars, which are mostly interpreted to mean "angels", in addition to causing havoc on earth. Thirdly, he has seven diadems, showing his great kingly ambition and inflated "self-identity". Fourthly, 11:9 clearly tells us that the dragon represents the ancient serpent, the devil and Satan, the adversary of God and of humanity, the arch tempter, slanderer and deceiver.

This particular vision seems to link back to the early days of creation when Satan was emboldened by his success in tempting Eve, leading Adam and Eve into sin and breaking their relationship with God. The action of the dragon here is often taken as a peek into how a fallen angel, who chose to be king instead of serving God the King, led other angels to follow him and started a full-scale opposition to God.

Anneke Kaai's painting imaginatively shows the woman, the dragon, and the battle to come, all in one image. I particularly like the way God embraces the baby and, with one and the same movement, protects the mother.

It took me a long time to decide how to portray the dragon. Our visual imaginations, heavily saturated by Disney, have mostly domesticated dragons. Smaug in The Hobbit films was impressive but, ultimately, I decided that the symbolism of the seven-headed serpent would be a better starting point. So, I returned to the classical idea of the Hydra and expanded that. My visualisation attempts to portray real, strong evil, ready to attack at all times, and from all sides.

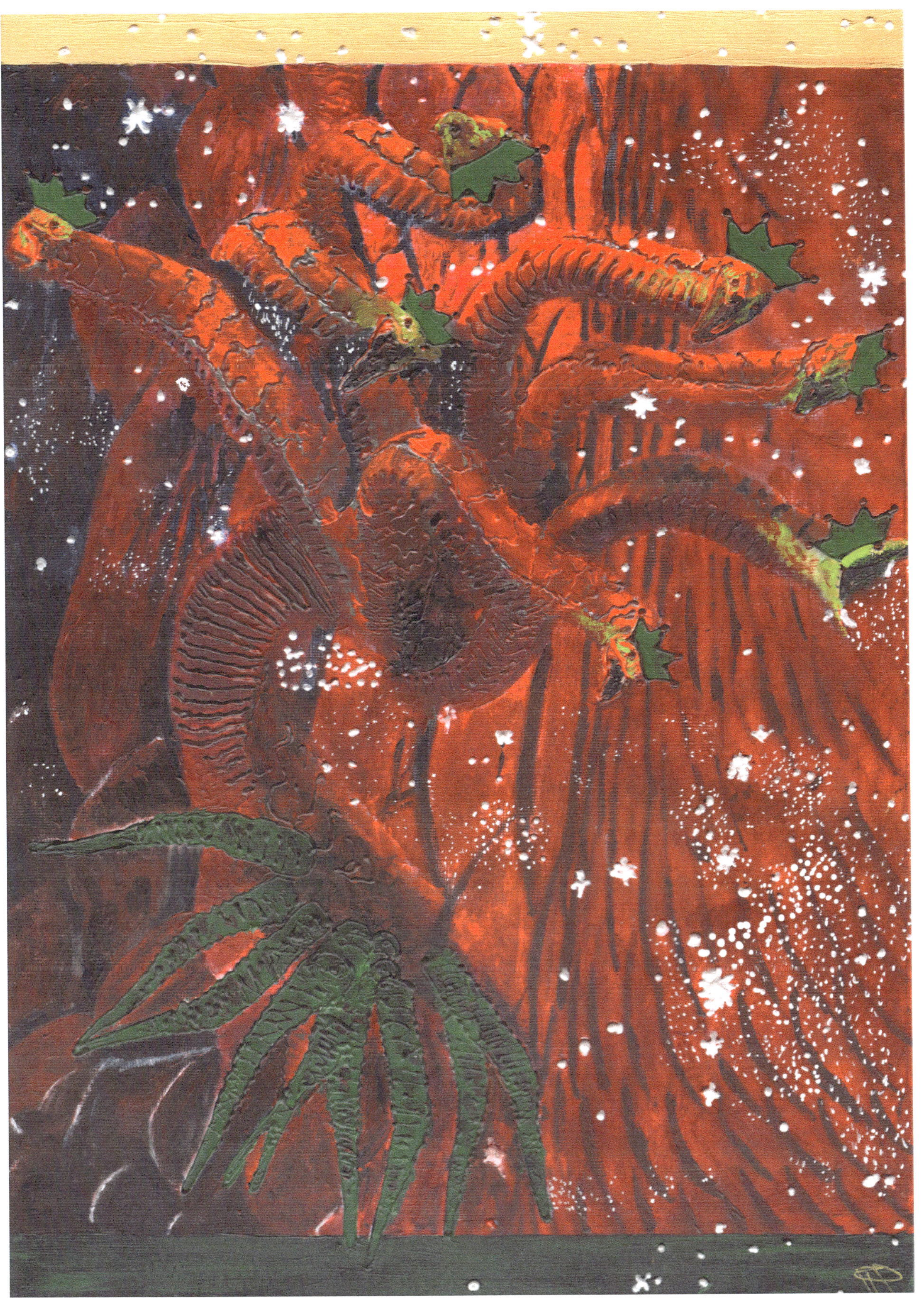

Enthronement

The action starts with the dragon threatening to devour the woman's child. This scene is depicted well in the Feibush lithograph below, which I quoted in my painting. The male child who is born turns out to be the true King who will rule all nations with an iron rod. But, in the vision the child is immediately snatched away and taken to God and His throne.

In my painting I have portrayed this vision with angels snatching the child up on God's behalf. The rod of iron cuts diagonally across the painting to create a distinct "barrier". The woman remains in glory as she gives birth.

What is happening here? Again, commentators are very divided. Some relate this to the birth of Jesus and his enthronement, but then must explain why the work and life of Jesus are so condensed. Others argue, like Caird, that this refers to the enthronement of Jesus, and that in light of Psalm 2 and Hebrews 1 this birth does not relate to His incarnation but to His birth into kingship. It explains why the crowned dragon wants to kill the child: the dragon sees in him a threat to the control of what it claims as its own domain. The dragon's fight with the woman, to get the child, is a clear reference to the prophecy in Genesis 3:

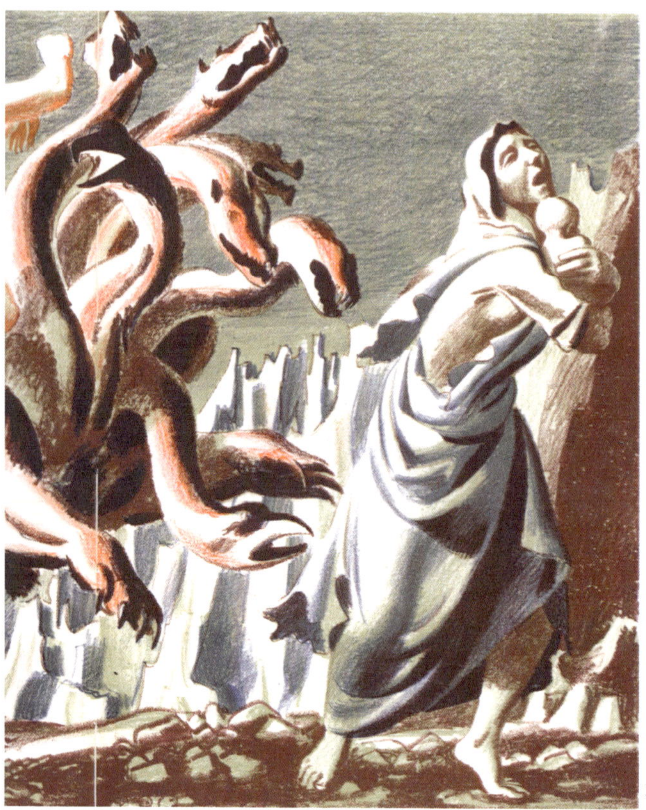

12: [4b]Then the dragon stood before the woman who was about to deliver a child, so that he might devour her child as soon as it was born. [5]And she gave birth to a son, a male child, who is to rule all the nations with a scepter of iron. But her child was snatched away and taken to God and to his throne.

[14]The LORD God said to the serpent, "Because you have done this, cursed are you among all animals and among all wild creatures; upon your belly you shall go, and dust you shall eat all the days of your life. I will put enmity between you and the woman, and between your offspring and hers; he will strike your head, and you will strike his heel."
To the woman he said, "I will greatly increase your pangs in childbearing; in pain you shall bring forth children..."

These verses from Genesis seem to form the background to everything being revealed to John in this vision. Often in Revelation, it is the Hebrew scriptures – about creation or the Pentateuch or the words of the prophets or specific Psalms – that John is apparently reminded of to make sense of what he sees. Here, from Psalm 2:

[7]I will tell of the decree of the LORD: He said to me, "You are my son; today I have begotten you. Ask of me, and I will make the nations your heritage, and the ends of the earth your possession. You shall break them with a rod of iron, and dash them in pieces like a potter's vessel."

In Hebrews 1:1–5, Psalm 2 is also quoted:

[1]Long ago God spoke to our ancestors in many and various ways by the prophets, but in these last days he has spoken to us by a Son, whom he appointed heir of all things, through whom he also created the worlds. He is the reflection of God's glory and the exact imprint of God's very being, and he sustains all things by his powerful word. When he had made purification for sins, he sat down at the right hand of the Majesty on high, having become as much superior to angels as the name he has inherited is more excellent than theirs. For to which of the angels did God ever say, "You are my Son; today I have begotten you"? Or again, "I will be his Father, and he will be my Son"? And again, when he brings the firstborn into the world, he says, "Let all God's angels worship him."

Jesus is finally enthroned, but, surprisingly, it is not yet the end of the action.

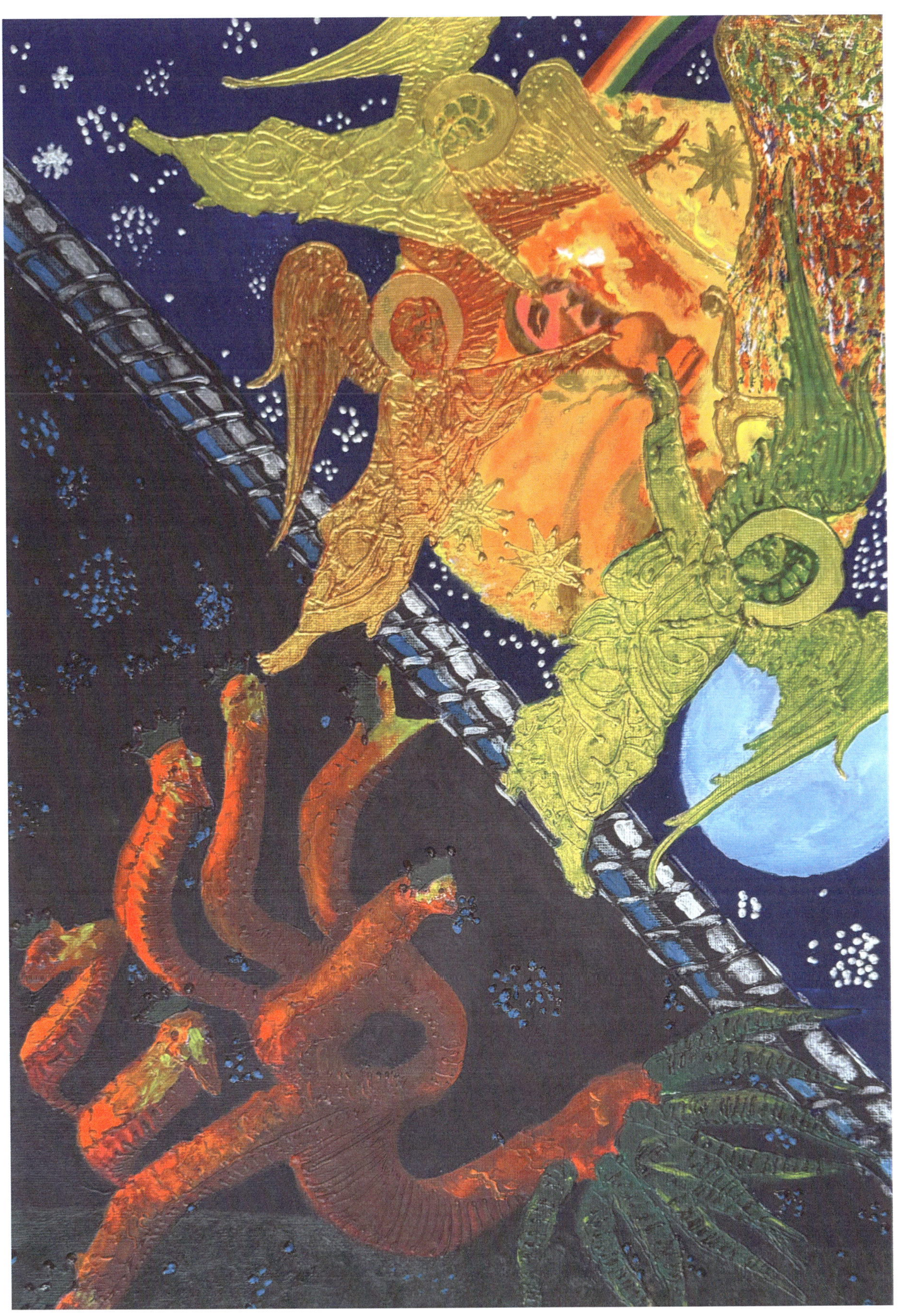

The Woman in the Wilderness

With God's help, the woman flees to the wilderness, where she will be nourished for 1,260 days. It demonstrates God's care for "Eve", and everyone she represents: Mary at the cross and God's people, both in OT times, in John's time and, by implication, today! God never stops caring for his people!

> *12: [6]and the woman fled into the wilderness, where she has a place prepared by God, so that there she can be nourished for one thousand two hundred sixty days.*

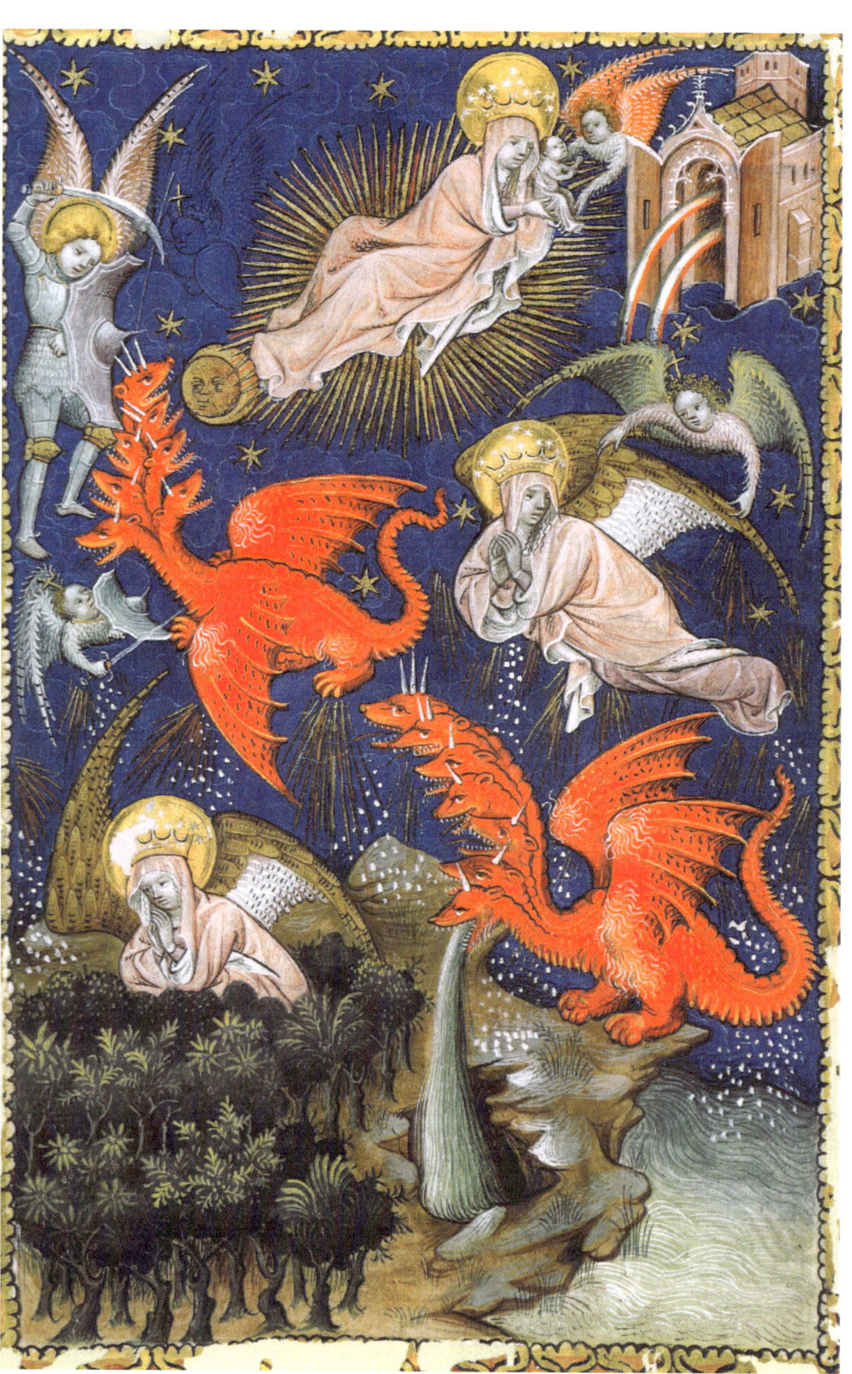

The "wilderness" reminds us of the many biblical events that take place in a wilderness, for example, Hagar's journey, the wandering people of Israel after the exodus, and so on. In Revelation, the exodus features in the other trumpet calls, so it is no surprise to find it here at the seventh and last call.

I painted the woman as sitting reading under the tree of life. She is experiencing some of her future glory in its shade. But on earth her place is now without any radiance of sun or moon. I added angels, too, but now just as a "memory", in the upper, golden, part. The number of days add up to 3.5 years (or "periods", elsewhere), as a sign that hardship comes for a specific period that God is aware of, and for which he has set limits. And, even though it may feel as if it is continuing, again and again, no end in sight, suddenly it ends!

I wanted to create a meditative and peaceful painting here. Another battle is coming, with threats and flight, but here, in this moment and place, the woman is completely at peace and nourished, despite the chaos at large.

The painting on the left, from the Flemish, tells the whole story of Revelation 12 in one image. It is worth taking time to look at it. There is much to see, and I love it! In the top right-hand corner, it portrays the ark in the temple, and everything else follows from that. The artist also uses an angel to snatch the child. This is visual storytelling at its best!

A particularly nice feature is the blue-clad angel, almost blending into the background, who is one of Michael's helpers. The next story will reveal more ...

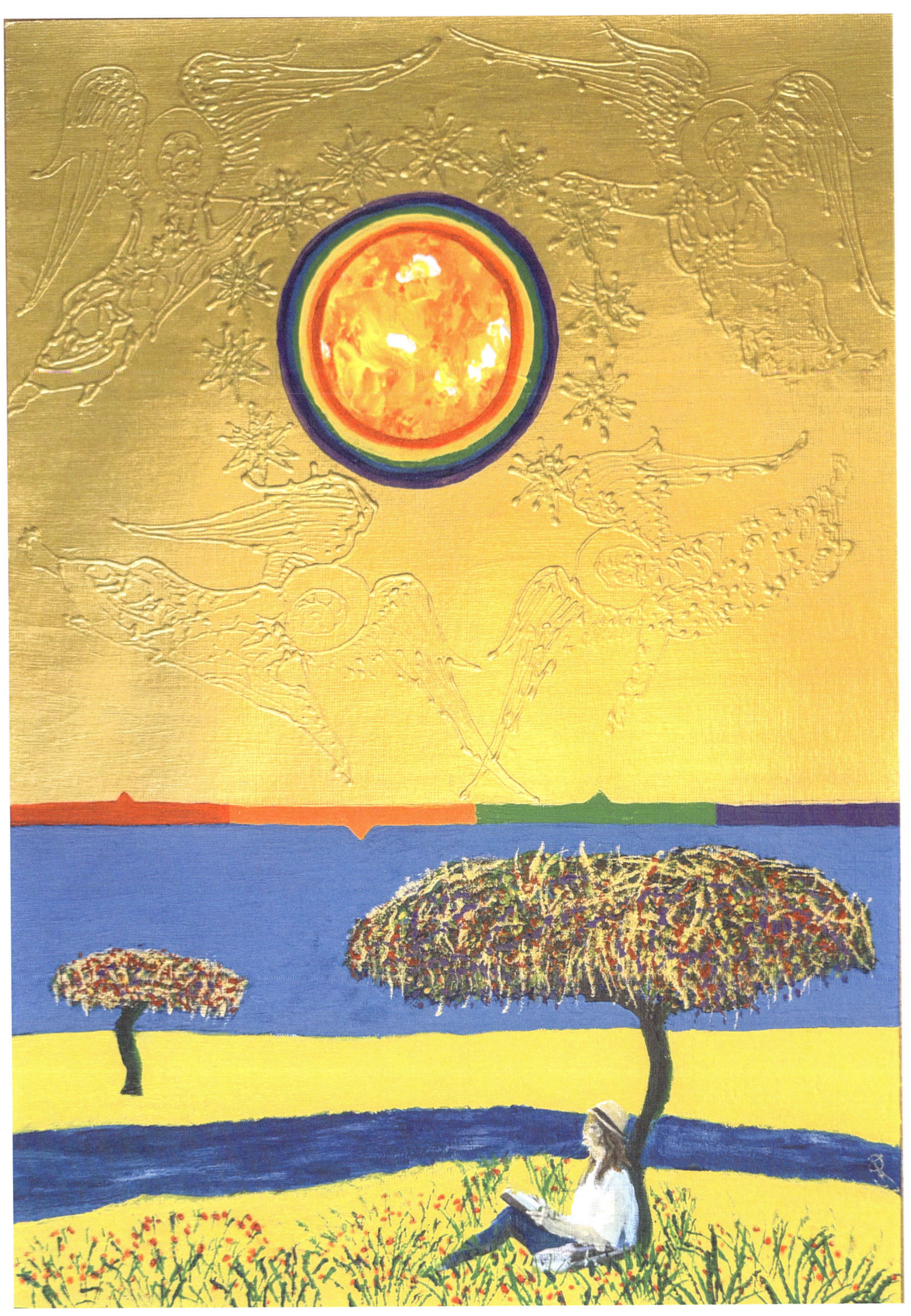

War in Heaven

Although peace reigns on earth, war has broken out in heaven. Michael is mentioned next, for the first and only time.

Who is Michael? His name means: "Who is like God!" Rather appropriate, as traditionally he is the archangel who looks after Israel (Dan 10:13, 21). In the NT an incident involving Michael is described in Jude 1:9:

But when the archangel Michael contended with the devil and disputed about the body of Moses, he did not dare to bring a condemnation of slander against him, but said, "The Lord rebuke you!"

From this, some commentators suggest that he closely identifies with Jesus and, in some cases, even that he is Jesus. I am not sure that is the case; it rather confuses his identity.

In medieval times, illustrators portrayed this war as being fought with real swords and spears, as can be seen in the Beatus illustration below. I find that too literal, believing that Revelation refers to spiritual warfare in the heavenlies.

Caird suggests that this is actually a courtroom battle in which Satan, as the accuser, is defeated and loses his place in heaven. He therefore signifies this story as the heavenly counterpart of the crucifixion. I think there is much to be said for this interpretation, especially when considering the doxology that follows.

12: [7]And war broke out in heaven; Michael and his
angels fought against the dragon. The dragon and
his angels fought back, [8]but they were defeated, and
there was no longer any place for them in heaven. [9]The
great dragon was thrown down, that ancient serpent,
who is called the devil and Satan, the deceiver of the
whole world – he was thrown down to the earth, and
his angels were thrown down with him.

The point is that the devil is thrown down to earth, where he becomes the deceiver of the world, roaming across the earth with his followers–presumably the fallen angels described when the devil swept down a third of the "stars".

In my painting, I tried to depict this ongoing legal and spiritual battle. The composition was inspired by Dürer's Michael. I portrayed the sword in a similar way to how I have done it in a number of previous paintings. I interpret it as the word of God, and previously showed it coming out of the mouth of the Lamb. The Lamb is very prominent here, with His blood being poured out. Under the sword, I have depicted deformed martyrs on earth. The light beam is my own addition, reflecting God's character in this battle. God is light, absorbing all colours into this pure white beam, which shines brightest in heaven but dimmer on earth (the green shadow). Satan is defeated and thrown down to earth.

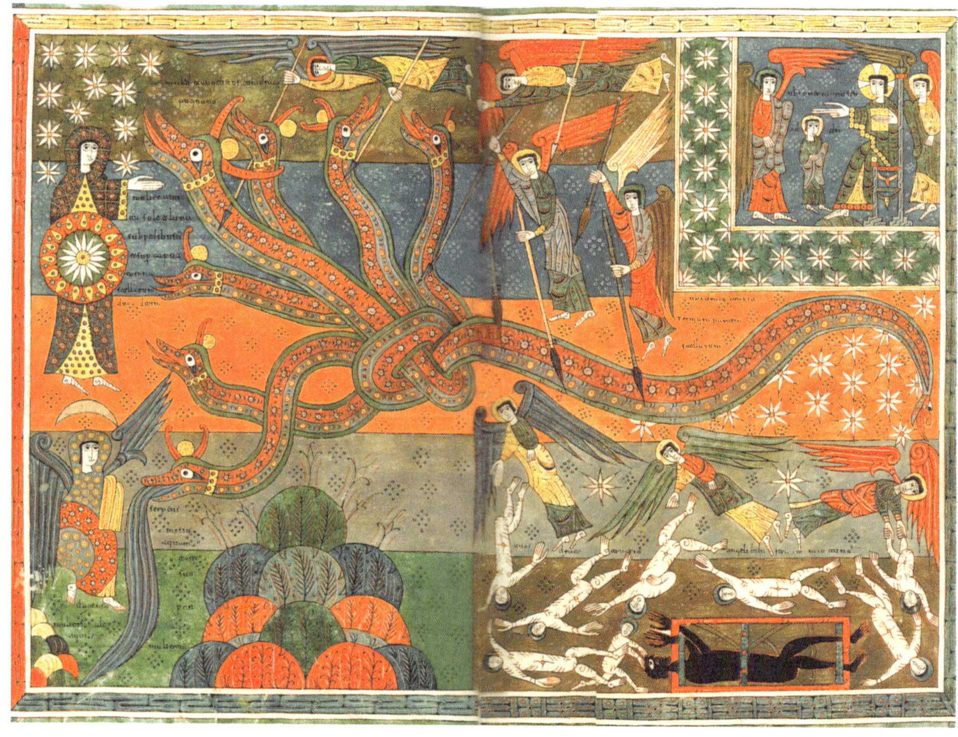

This painting has taken me a long time to complete after meditating on the spiritual battle for more than a year. During that time, the battle felt very real in my own life.

The painting seeks to show that the battle in heaven immediately and directly affects earth. I believe this is very clear in the story. And the battle is primarily a spiritual one!

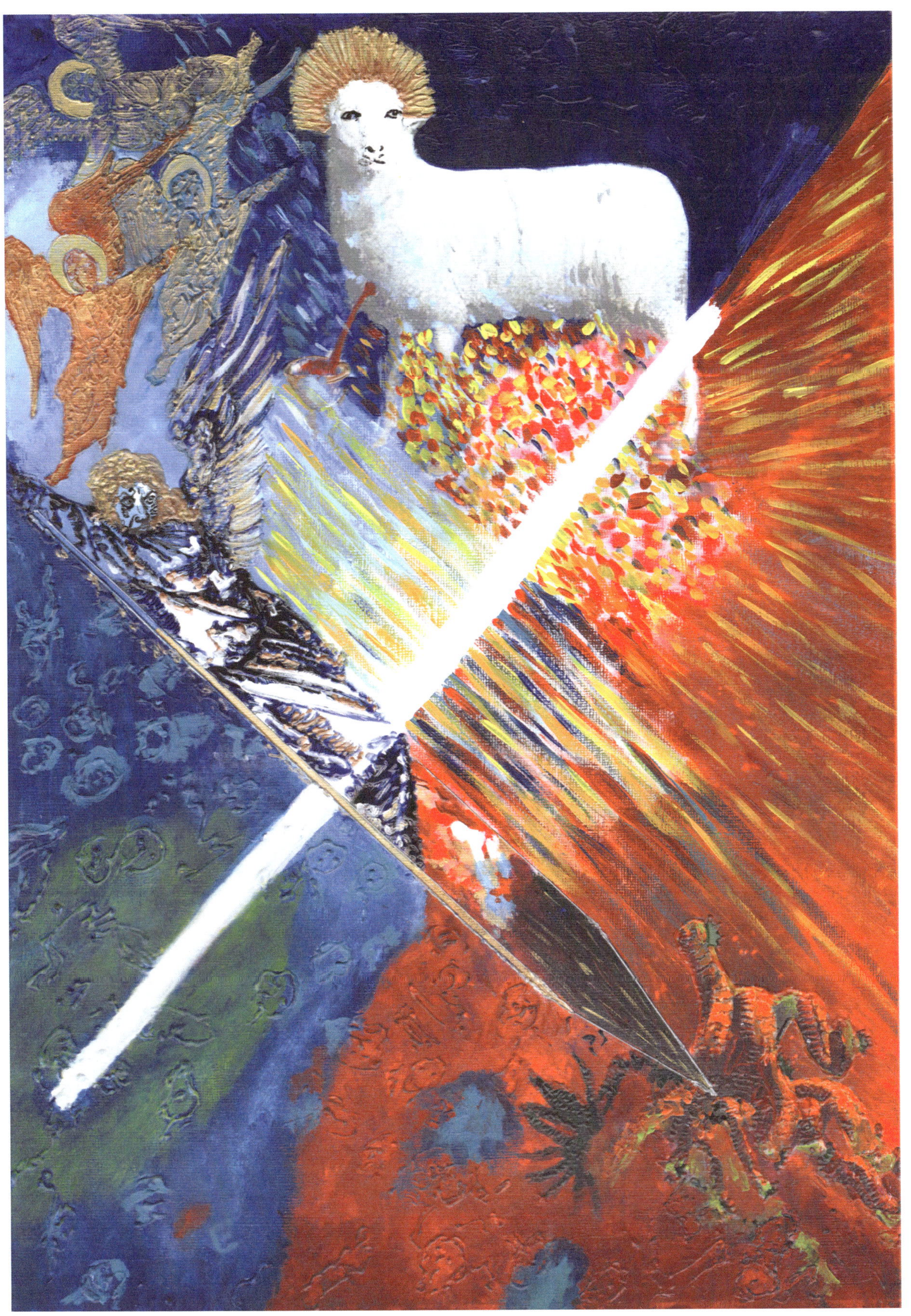

They Conquered, Woe to Earth and Sea

John sees a celebration in heaven and hears a proclamation that sounds very much like the one at the opening of the seventh trumpet (11:11). The fall of Satan is linked with the coming of the kingdom of the Messiah. This liturgy refers to the conclusion of the war in heaven John just witnessed. The proclamation adds that this war was won not by Michael alone, but also by Christian martyrs who triumphed by the blood of the Lamb and by their testimony. It is an amazing victory for Christ and for the churches, and a reason to rejoice! But, woe to the earth and the sea ...

12: [10]Then I heard a loud voice in heaven proclaiming,
"Now have come the salvation and the power and the
kingdom of our God and the authority of his Messi-
ah, for the accuser of our brothers and sisters has been
thrown down, who accuses them day and night before
our God. [11]But they have conquered him by the blood of
the Lamb and by the word of their testimony, for they
did not cling to life even in the face of death. [12]Rejoice
then, you heavens and those who dwell in them! But
woe to the earth and the sea, for the devil has come
down to you with great wrath because he knows that
his time is short!"

The big question is, is this is the third woe? Although some commentators have their doubts, I agree with the majority that this is indeed the "third woe", still part of the seventh trumpet. It is the final "woe" in a trilogy of woes, as will be clear in what follows.

In the past, this passage has not received much attention from illustrators. In fact, I found only one, in the *Picture Book of the Life of St John and the Apocalypse*, which can be seen below. It shows two angels holding up the Latin text of Revelation 12:10, which was abbreviated, leaving significant space to spare below the text. The tree with the bird's nest to the right seems a strange addition?

In my own painting, I express the true joy of heaven at the top, with the Lamb of God at the centre. Beatus angels and my granddaughter's angels circle around him in celebration. Again, I use the motif of the trumpet to indicate a loud voice. I have also referred to some Naga evangelists whom I had met and who embodied so clearly how true witness comes from faith-fully lived lives! And, I have included a Ukrainian martyr, a medic on the frontline at the time of his death. I show him now, celebrating with the angels in heaven, his life "fulfilled".

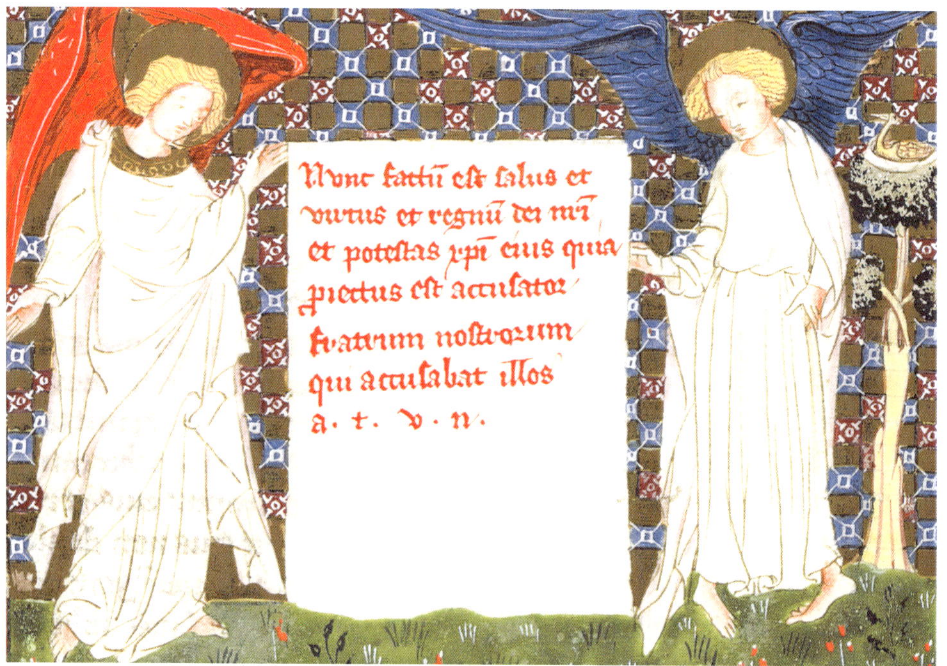

The rod of iron with which the Lamb rules the earth and its nations separates the top and bottom halves. Below, Satan and his followers pollute the earth and sea with their deception, lies, fake news and propaganda.

So, the lines of the battle are clearly drawn. The days of repentance are coming to an end. Will this woe bring the final destruction of all the evil powers and those who follow and worship them? The vision continues ...

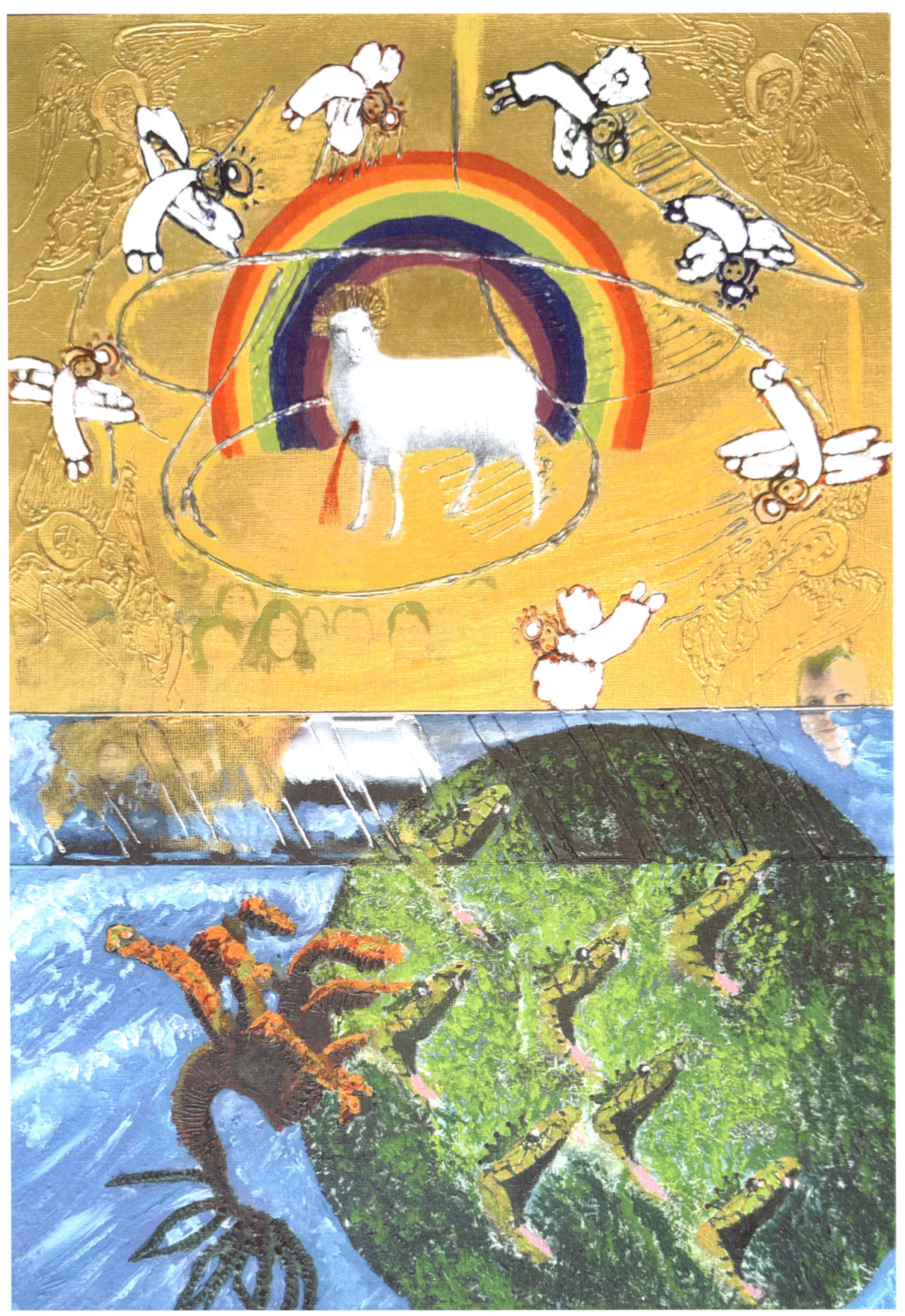

A Hot Pursuit

But what about the woman? Will she be subject to this woe? Not directly, for she is being given the wings of an eagle/vulture. Swete suggests that this is most likely the griffin vulture, and I have taken that as my lead for painting.

And what about the serpent? Wild with anger, he now has only one aim: to destroy the woman, who represents God's unshakeable commitment also to the earth. Satan wants to destroy humanity, and more specifically the church, the rest of her children: those who keep God's commandments and bear witness to Jesus.

The battle then moves to earth and, though the war has already been won in heaven, much damage can still be inflicted between "D-day" and "V-day". The serpent opens his mouth and pours water after the woman – a kind of fake flood? – but, unlike what happened during the biblical flood, the earth responds by opening its "mouth" and swallowing the flood! Is this a surprising reversal of God's curse on humanity in Adam, that the earth will no longer be "for them"? And if so, is this to Satan an unexpected revelation of God's outrageous mercy, that nevertheless the earth swallows the flood unlike Genesis 6?

*12: 13So when the dragon saw that he had been thrown
down to the earth, he pursued the woman who had
delivered the male child. 14But the woman was given
the two wings of the great eagle, so that she could fly
from the serpent into the wilderness, to her place where
she is nourished for a time, and times, and half a time.
15Then from his mouth the serpent poured water like
a river after the woman, to sweep her away with the
flood. 16But the earth came to the help of the woman;
it opened its mouth and swallowed the river that the
dragon had poured from his mouth. 17Then the dragon
was angry with the woman and went off to wage war
on the rest of her children, those who keep the commandments of God and hold the testimony of Jesus.*

The Val-Dieu painting below clearly depicts this.

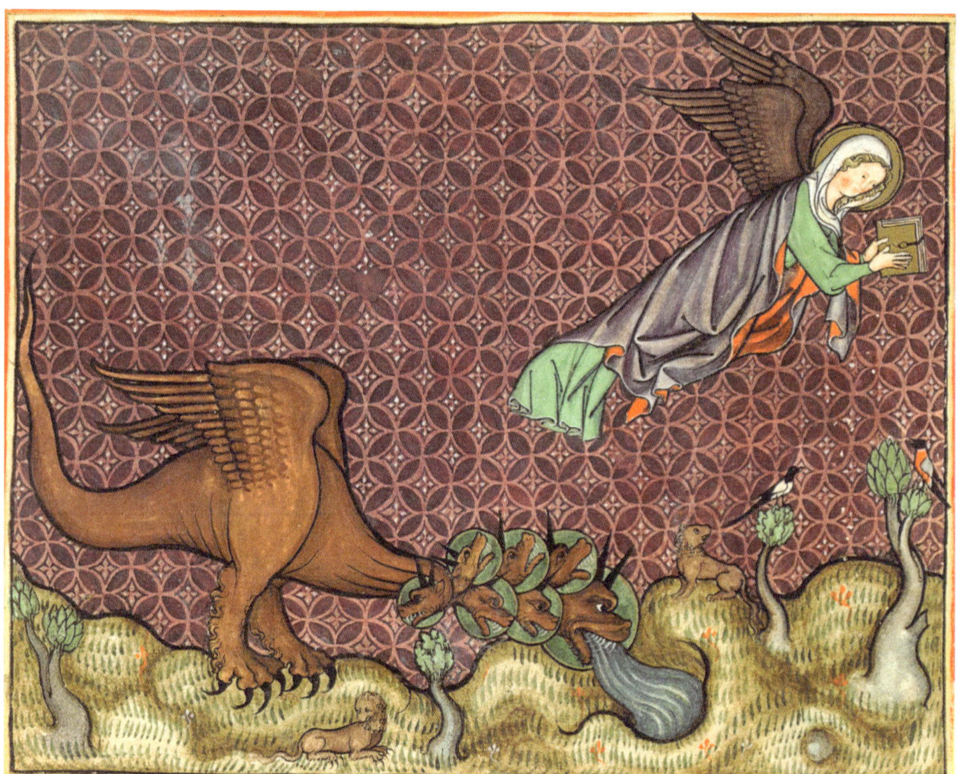

In my own painting, I depict the water and the serpent both rushing at the woman, who flies away towards the tree of life. I painted the earth in gold because it is clearly aligned with God in helping the woman. I depicted the rest of the woman's children as a flock of eagles in the heavenly sky. The water symbolises the multitude of deceptions that come from the dragon's mouth.

I divide my painting with a timeline, as used before, to show God in control of time and in control of what happens in time. Most importantly, here, God is actively protecting his people.

So, what is promised in this vision? That the church will endure; and in extremity may even be given eagle wings (Isa 40:31)! The dragon, in the meantime, is not ready to capitulate.

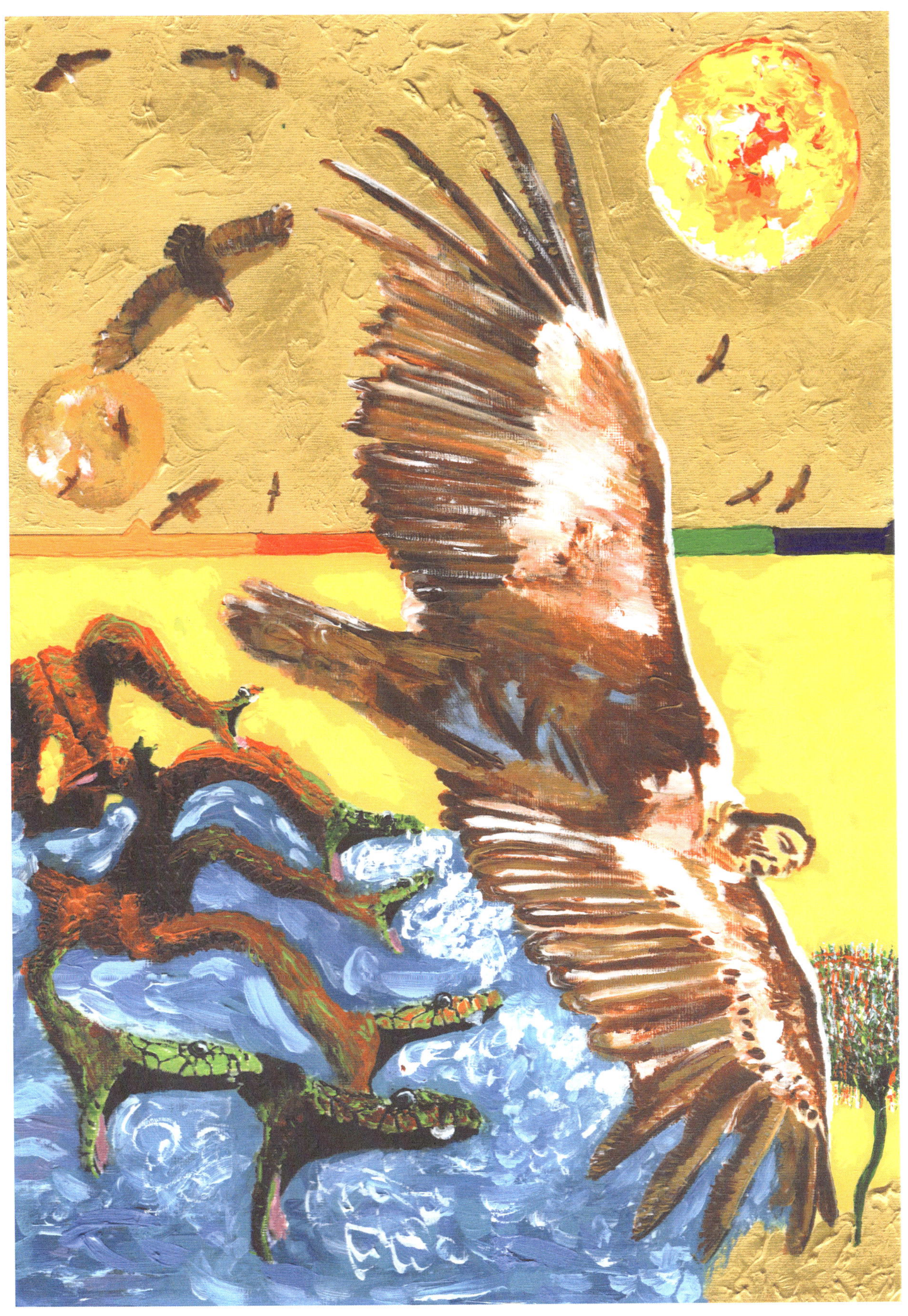

The Beast from the Sea

The dragon and his beast have similar authority, with the same number of horns and heads, though the beast has more diadems and looks like a composite of the first three beasts in Daniel 7: a lion, a bear and a leopard.

The whole story of this chapter is depicted in vivid images and colours in the Flemish below. It reads from top to bottom, starting with the dragon handing over his authority to the beast. Significantly, this is all happening under the watchful eye of God/Jesus. I like that.

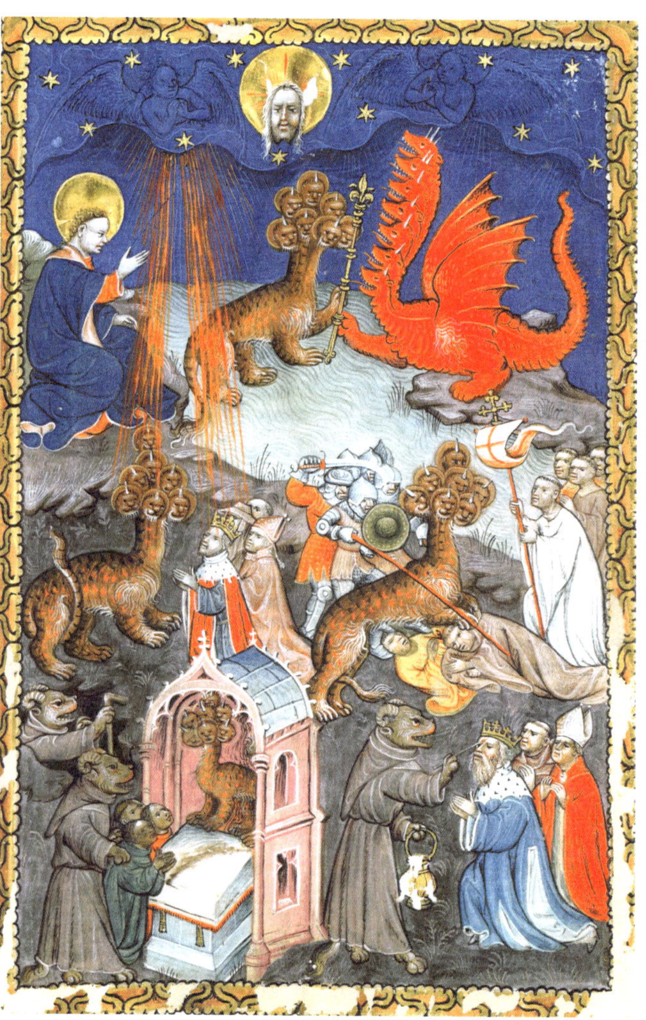

12: [18]Then the dragon took his stand on the sand of the seashore.

13: [1]And I saw a beast rising out of the sea, with ten horns and seven heads, and on its horns were ten diadems, and on its heads were blasphemous names. [2]And the beast that I saw was like a leopard, its feet were like a bear's, and its mouth was like a lion's mouth. And the dragon gave it his power and his throne and great authority. [3]One of its heads seemed to have received a death blow, but its fatal wound had been healed. In amazement the whole earth followed the beast.

In my own painting of this passage, I made sure that the golden presence heads up the painting. Along the sides, I placed sidebars representing 42 months (12:5). The dragon stands on the earth while the beast arises from the sea. The beast is depicted with claws, heads, teeth, skin and blasphemous names. The throne in the centre symbolises the transfer of the dragon's authority to the beast.

But who is the beast? Many scholars are quick to provide a very specific answer. Some suggest the Roman Empire and consider the matter closed. Others suggest it is a person, the antiChrist, although John never uses this name for the beast. But he was given a full name for the dragon. Some suggest the beast symbolises political power, while others think it refers to the power of the Roman Catholic Church. Still others think it is a person or anti-Christian system yet to be revealed.

The open scroll reveals the nature of God's adversary on earth: a beast, ferocious and dangerous. It is an incarnation on earth of Satan, a powerful pretender, a composite creature and a blasphemer. This beast is second in the evil trinity. His power comes from the dragon. One of his heads received a mortal wound but it was healed, which gave him worldwide and charismatic power as a leader.

I sense power like that at work today, and constantly being revealed as having been at work in the past, in leaders and leadership structures at every level ...

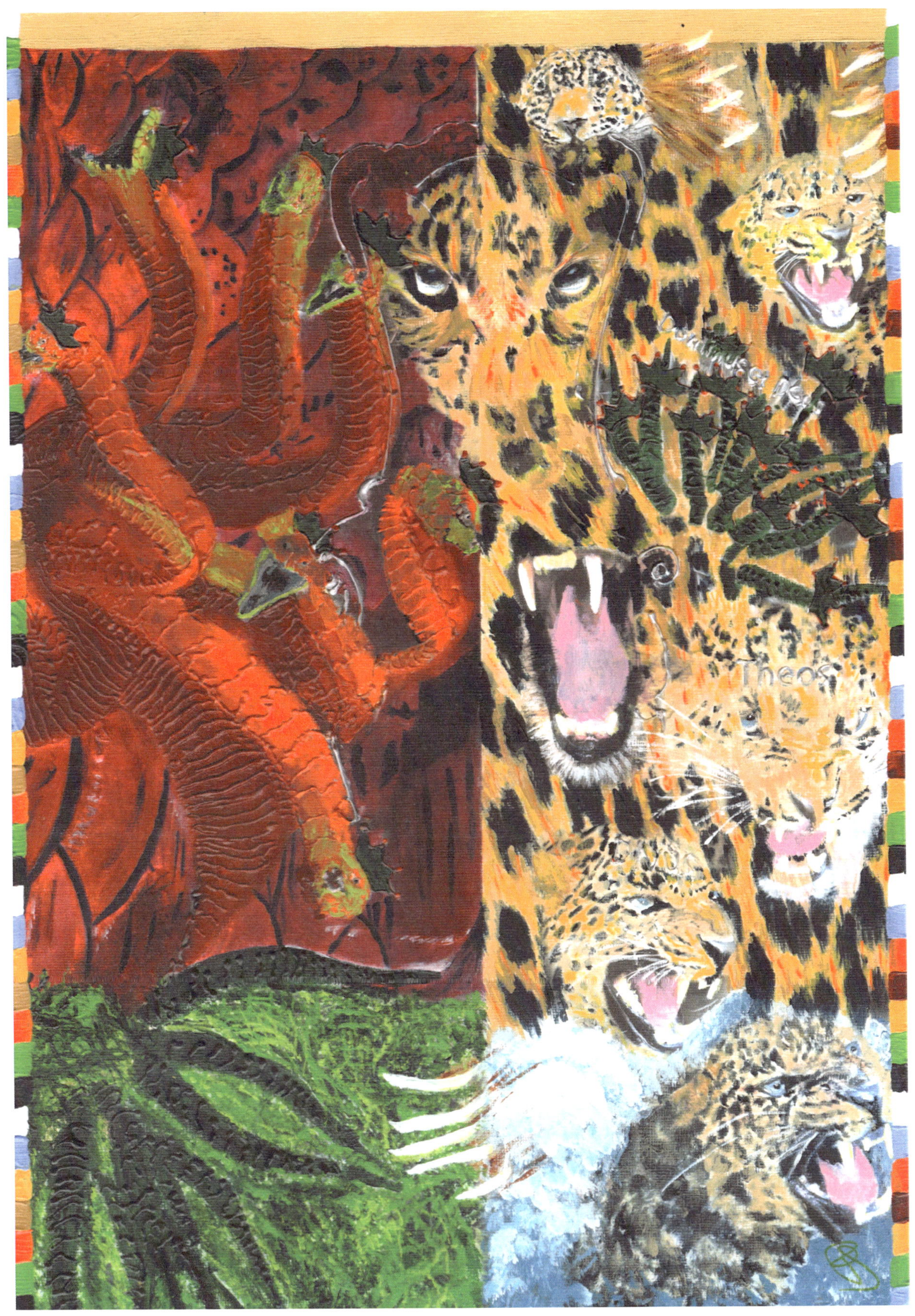
Theos

Worship of the Beast

The whole earth follows the beast in awe. "Who is like the beast" parodies "who is like God", the name of "Michael" who has defeated God's attackers in heaven. That defeat makes a mockery of the beast's self-entitlement, which implies no one can fight the beast?

In amazement the whole earth followed the beast.
4They worshiped the dragon, for he had given his authority to the beast, and they worshiped the beast, saying, "Who is like the beast, and who can fight against it?"
5The beast was given a mouth speaking arrogant and blasphemous words, and it was allowed to exercise authority for forty-two months.
6It opened its mouth to speak blasphemies against God, blaspheming his name and his dwelling, that is, those who dwell in heaven.
7Also, it was allowed to wage war on the saints and to conquer them. It was given authority over every tribe and people and language and nation,
8and all the inhabitants of the earth will worship it, everyone whose name has not been written from the foundation of the world in the book of life of the Lamb that was slaughtered.

The Val-Dieu illustration is a literal depiction of the worship of the dragon and the beast, closer to the text than my own, for I depict only the beast and represent him only by one of his heads. My painting alludes to worshippers of all ethnicities and religious backgrounds. In the right bottom corner, I include a "fragment" of the Lamb's book of Life (the biblical text here refers to those not written in it). Everything described here is happening on earth.

When artists depict the beast, they need to create an image that is both frightening and attractive. The beast clearly has great appeal. He is the arch-imitation, the counterfeit, the proud usurper, the great liar who makes (and apparently believes) his own created reality.

It's not hard to find examples of this beastly power at work today: world leaders worshipped by the church and the world; systems of technology and technological products that are worshipped; and so on.

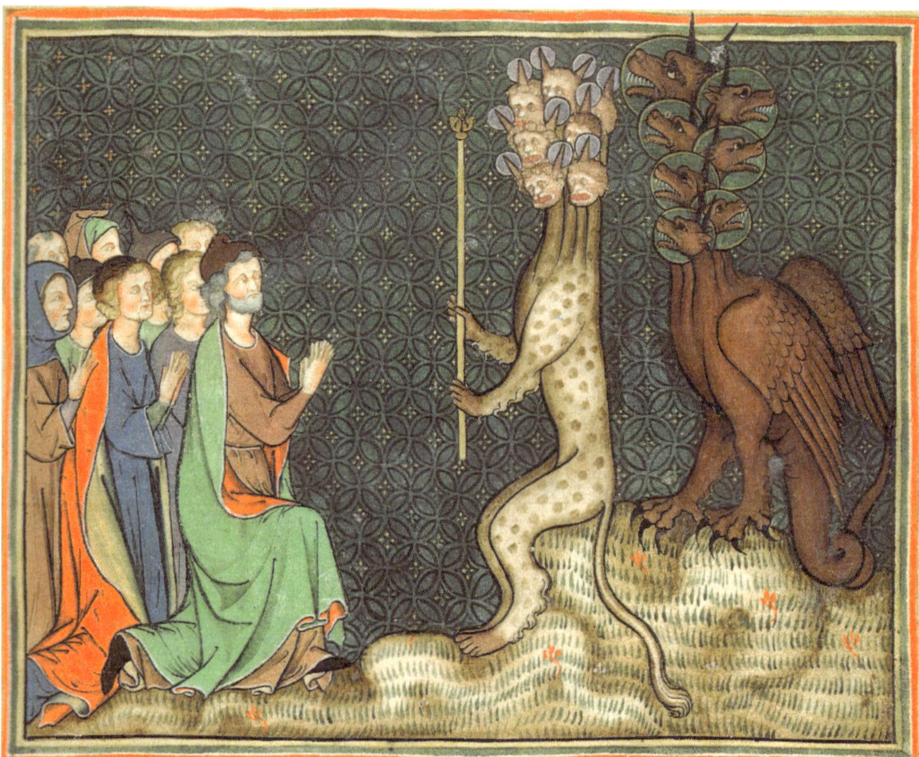

Not just God but also those in heaven are blasphemed. And, God apparently "allows" the beast to make war on the saints and to conquer them (12:7; also in 11:7 already)! As a result, the beast is worshipped by those from every tribe, people, language and nation ...

The "blasphemy against heaven" here is difficult to depict visually. As I could not find any examples of the ancients attempting it, neither did I.

For me, the key messages from meditating on this text in order to paint it has been the introduction of an opponent that is revealed to have real and overwhelming power to conquer, beyond our power to oppose. A scary prospect for those considering resistance ... and, exactly the intended outcome?

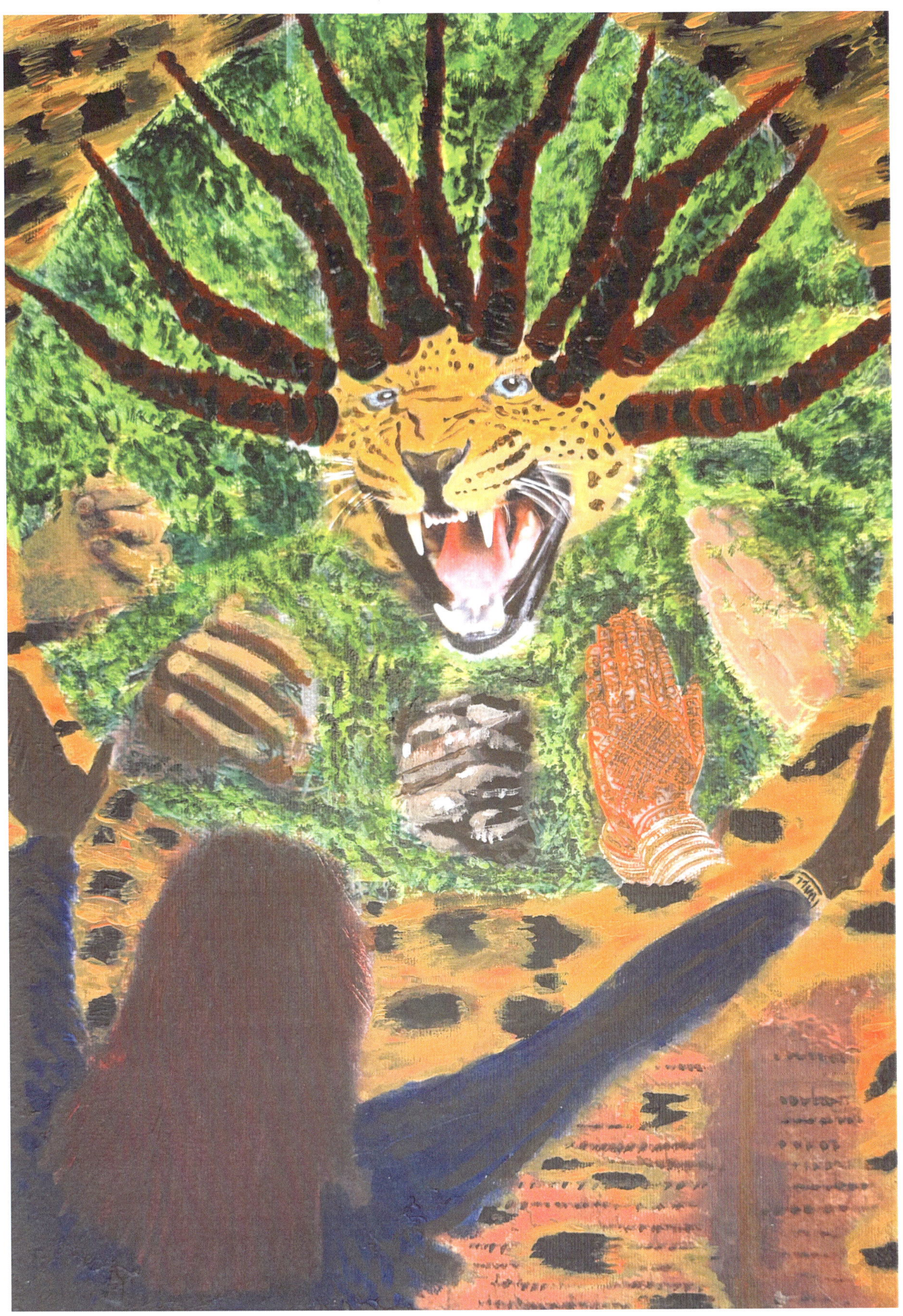

A Call to Endurance and Faith

Amidst this terrifying revelation, we are reminded that if we have ears, we must listen! I initially considered painting a large ear, but decided against it. (Spiritual "hearing" is not dependent on physical ears of flesh!) Instead, I was reminded of the church in Smyrna, the suffering church that has the cross as its symbol. So, I painted it in gold to represent the presence of God, with white to represent the saints and red to represent the martyrs. A dragon hovers threateningly behind it, taking some and killing many, but "swords", which I take to have a double meaning in these verses, are equally hard at work below, cutting down the beast.

It is good to be reminded that Revelation was addressed to the church as a whole, as well as to her individual members. This revelation of evil is for their benefit, as warning and encouragement. It was not given to arouse gloating or fear but to show that God is faithfully engaged and has the plan, as it often does not feel like that in daily life on earth.

None of the ancient manuscripts attempt to depict this endurance. So, I inserted a painting from the Luther Bible here that shows the Sea beast and the Land beast [which we will meet in the next Story]. During the Reformation, the beasts were identified as being aligned to the Roman Catholic Church, and the office of the pope was seen as essentially anti-Christian because of its oppressive alliances and power.

13: [9]Let anyone who has an ear listen: [10]If you are to be taken captive, into captivity you go; if you kill with the sword, with the sword you must be killed. Here is a call for the endurance and faith of the saints.

In my opinion, these verses are key for those addressed by Jesus: a call to endurance and faith! Not curiosity about what may happen next or excessive interest in the details about the beasts, but a sober acknowledgement of their beastliness and an encouragement for those who struggle against them and who may die at their hands!

I painted this painting while travelling and feeling greatly stressed by a systematic and biblical theology of evil I was reading and found hard to digest at the time.

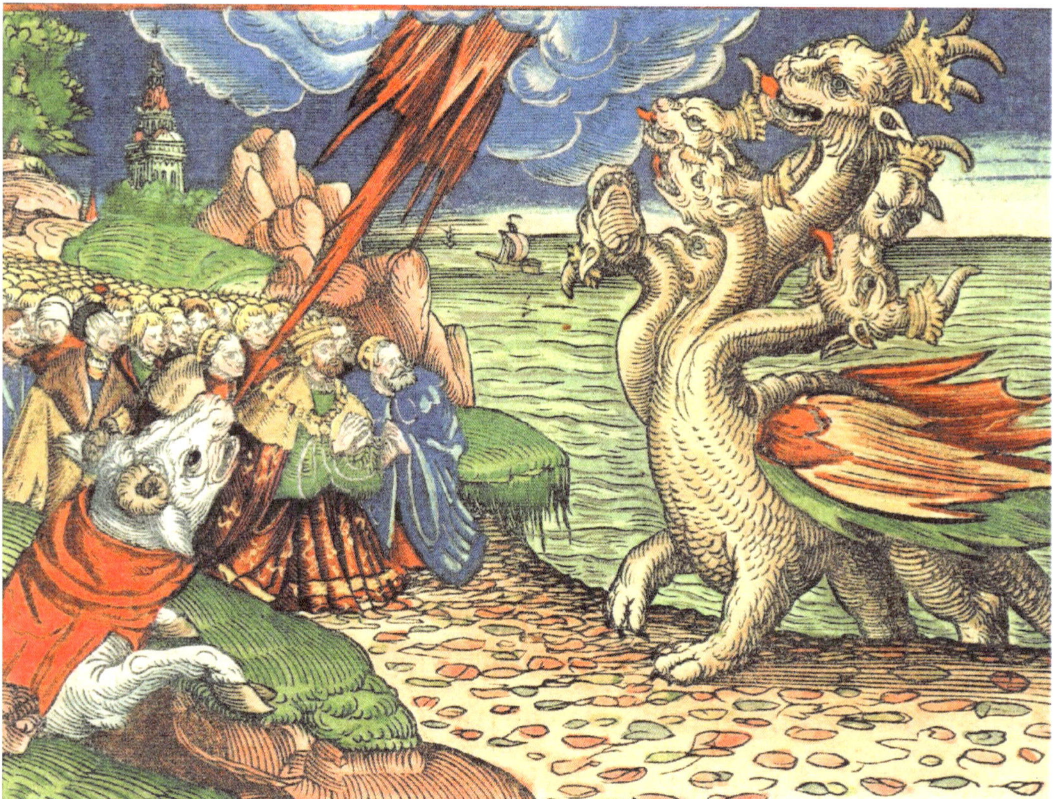

Over 1,000 pages in, it struck me that Scripture does not devote nearly as much attention to the origin of evil as such books do ...

Painting this became a joy, an overcoming and a healing as I remembered that Revelation is a revelation by, from and about Jesus! Seeing it, I came to know Him better! His person becomes clearer when I saw His counterfeits, who are no match for Him as this book continues to state in no uncertain terms. His Church will stand. She will tremble, suffer and die, but then she will live!

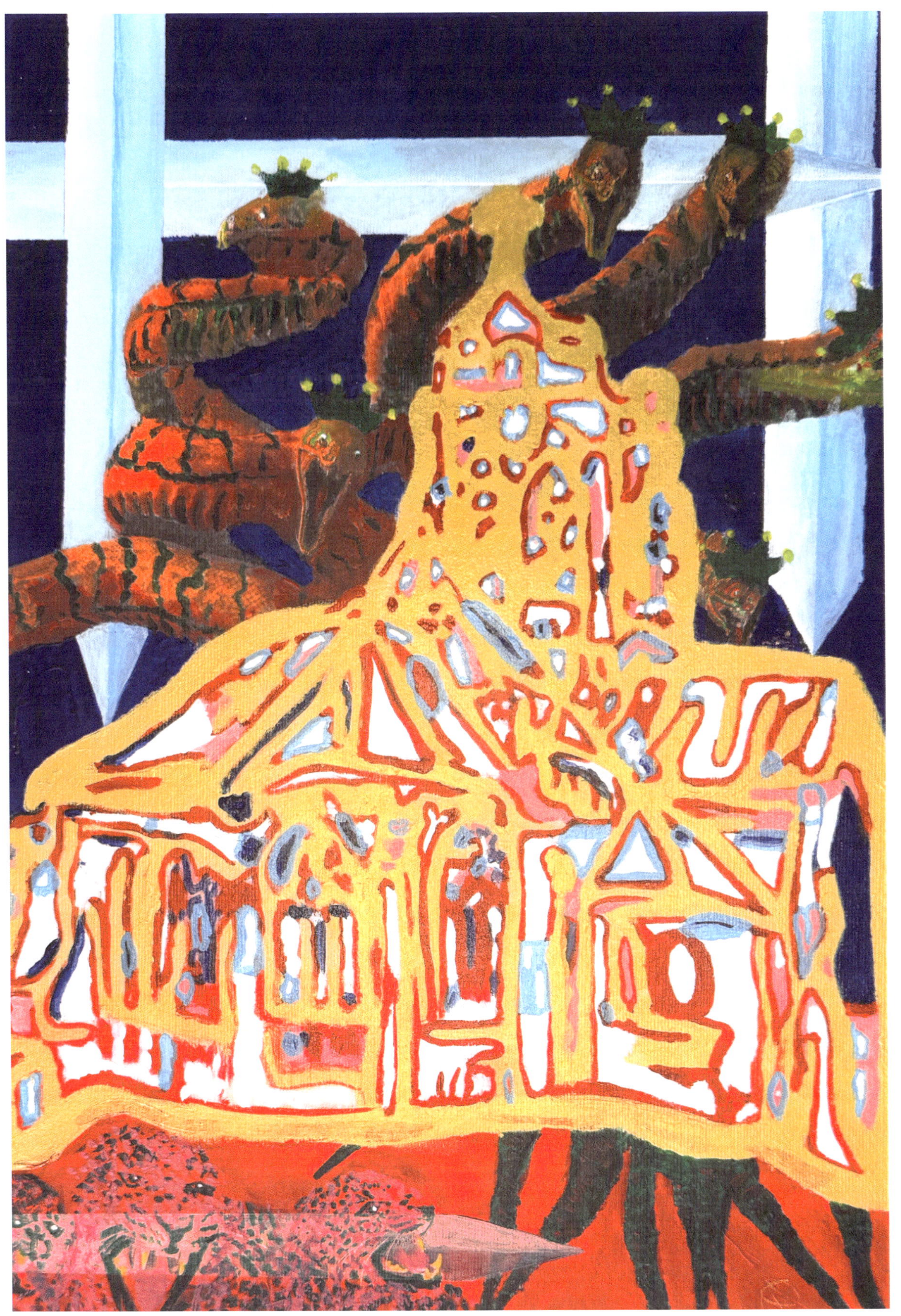

The Beast from the Earth

The dragon does not stop at one beast. Next John sees a beast rising from the earth that looks like a lamb with two horns. But he speaks like the dragon. It is his ability to speak that makes this lamb so dangerous. Like the dragon, he has great authority, and he is intent on making the inhabitants of the earth worship the Sea beast, whose mortal wound has been healed.

13: [11]Then I saw another beast that rose out of the earth: it had two horns like a lamb, and it spoke like a dragon. [12]It exercises all the authority of the first beast on its behalf, and it makes the earth and its inhabitants worship the first beast, whose fatal wound had been healed. [13]It performs great signs, even making fire come down from heaven to earth in the sight of all; ...

Who is this second beast? He seems to be a religious beast and will later be called a "false prophet" – a beast arising out of the people of God, because people outside the covenant community were never referred to as false prophets? But it is better not to equate this beast with one particular person. This kind of "prophet" can be identified in every age since the ascension of Jesus. Many in the church have performed signs or made great claims, while promoting gods or ideas alien to the triune God of the Scriptures and his teaching.

The Val-Dieu goes beyond the description of the beast of the Land. It adds claws and makes this lamb look like a ram. However, it is clearly directing fire towards those who do not worship the Sea beast.

In my painting I depicted fireworks. And I painted a large lamb with a serpent's mouth standing on a serpent-filled earth. I wanted to express the sense of a complete takeover.

In my research, however, I could not find any images of lambs with horns on their heads. It reminded me that Revelation must never be taken too literally!

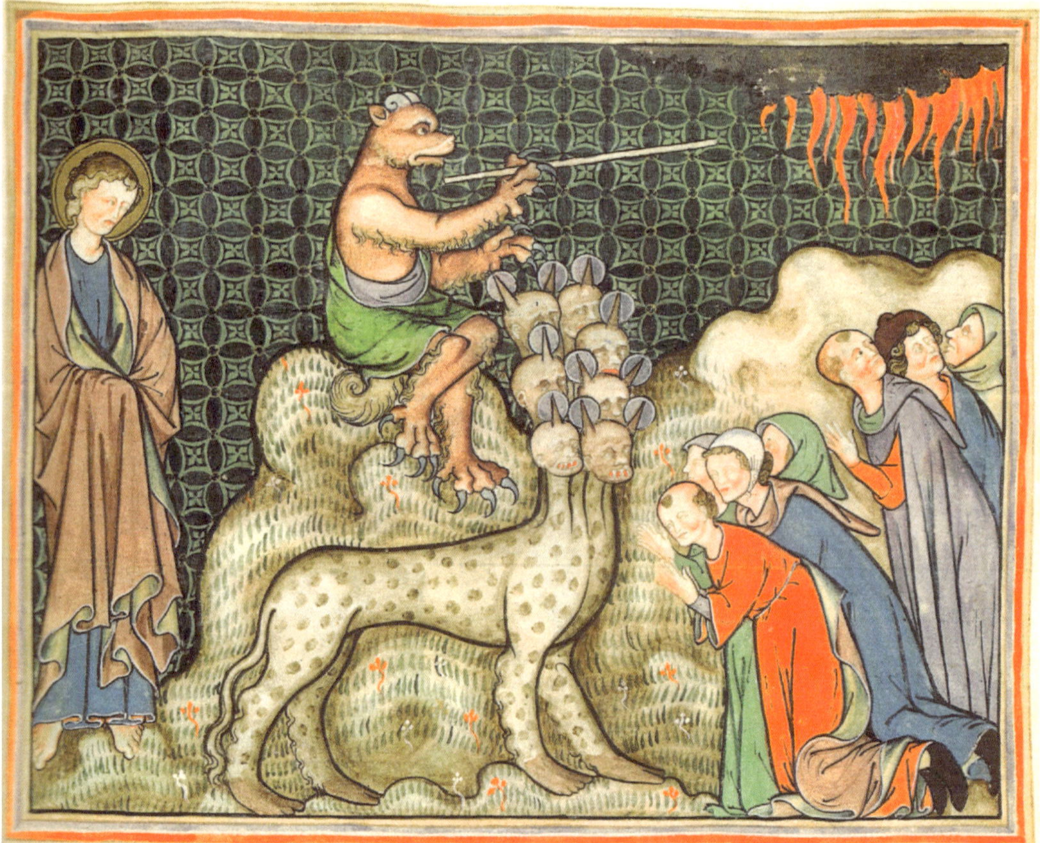

But the combination of false speech and counterfeit cuteness to project innocence that this lamb has, is something I can find readily in our own culture today. And when I do, I am reminded not to focus too intently on the individual. Instead, I pray against this "false" spirit that is powerfully active, also today, and particularly directed against those within the church!

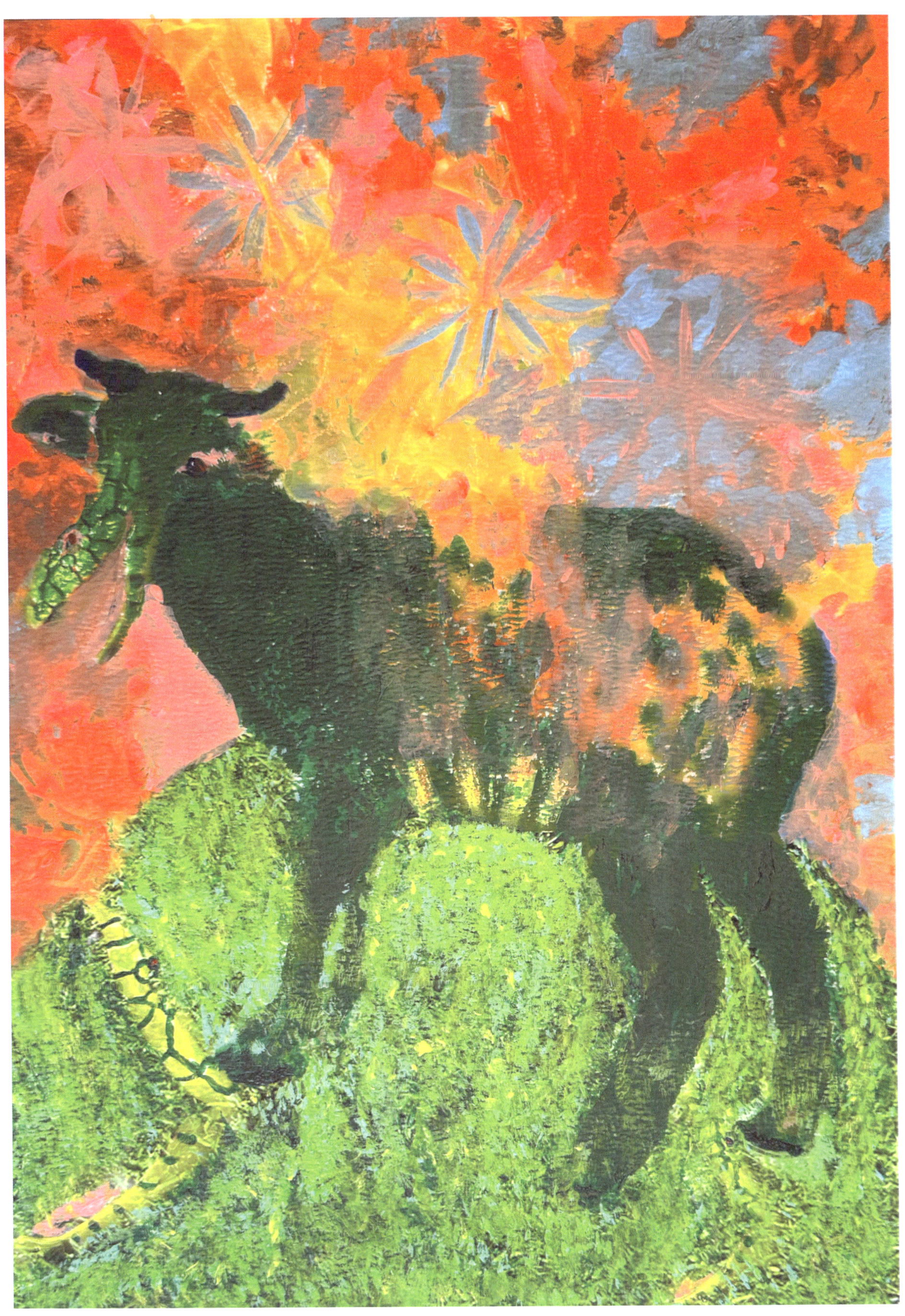

Worship the Image of the Beast

The signs are intended to deceive; the fire from heaven is reminiscent of the priests of Baal and Elijah. God answered Elijah; now, God allows these miracles to be performed by the land beast.

Why make an image of the sea beast? An image is a red flag to all true believers who remember the second commandment: "You shall not make for yourself an image of anything."

They should also remember the passage in Deuteronomy that any prophet who performs miracles such as fire from heaven or making statues speak, but who leads us to follow other gods, is anathema, and they should continue to follow God.

The prophets of the Old Testament were also adamant that these images made of wood, stone or technology, such as robots, are deceptive.

We also enter the realm of Daniel's account of Nebuchadnezzar, who had a statue made and forced everyone to worship it or be killed.

13: [14]and by the signs that it is allowed to perform on behalf of the beast it deceives the inhabitants of earth, telling them to make an image for the beast that had been wounded by the sword and yet lived; [15]and it was allowed to give breath to the image of the beast so that the image of the beast could even speak and cause those who would not worship the image of the beast to be killed.

This is graphically depicted in the Val-Dieu image.

In my painting, I focus on the miracle of the statue speaking, which I believe to be real rather than fake. I also depict the multitude worshipping at the land beast's encouragement.

I do not depict the threat of death. In painting, we make our choices.

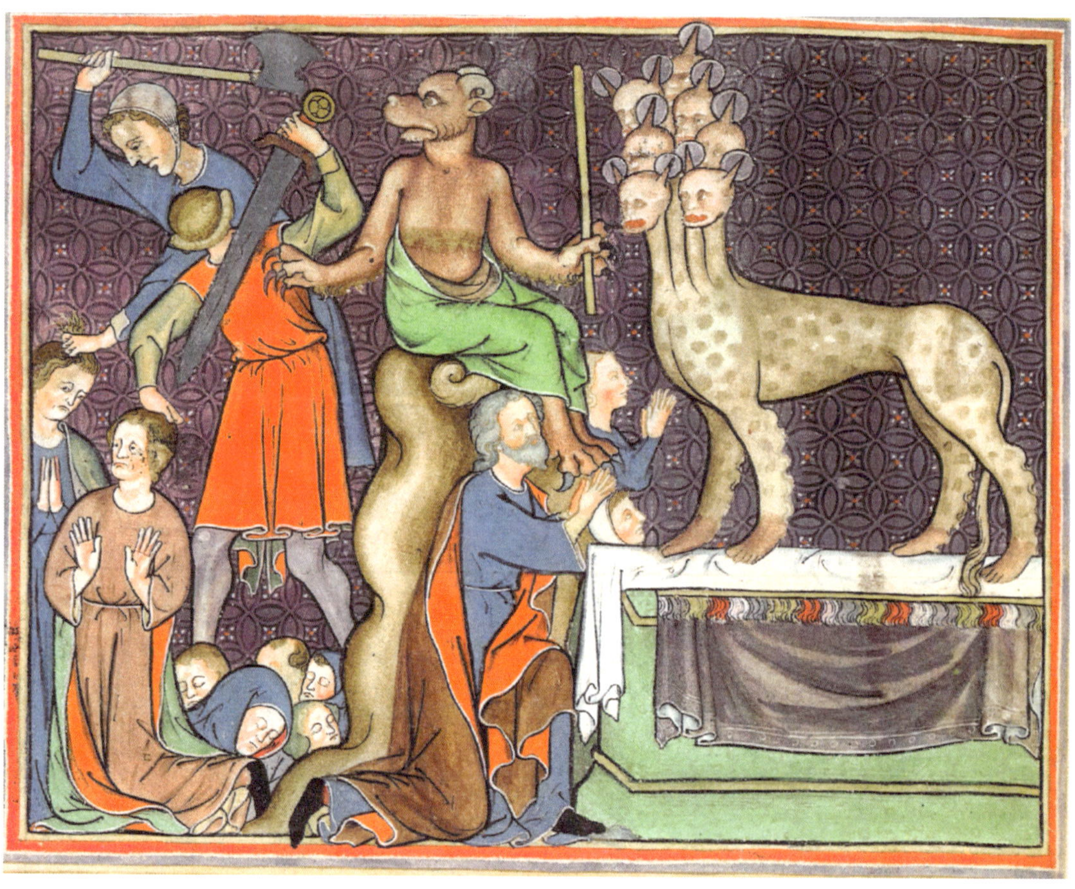

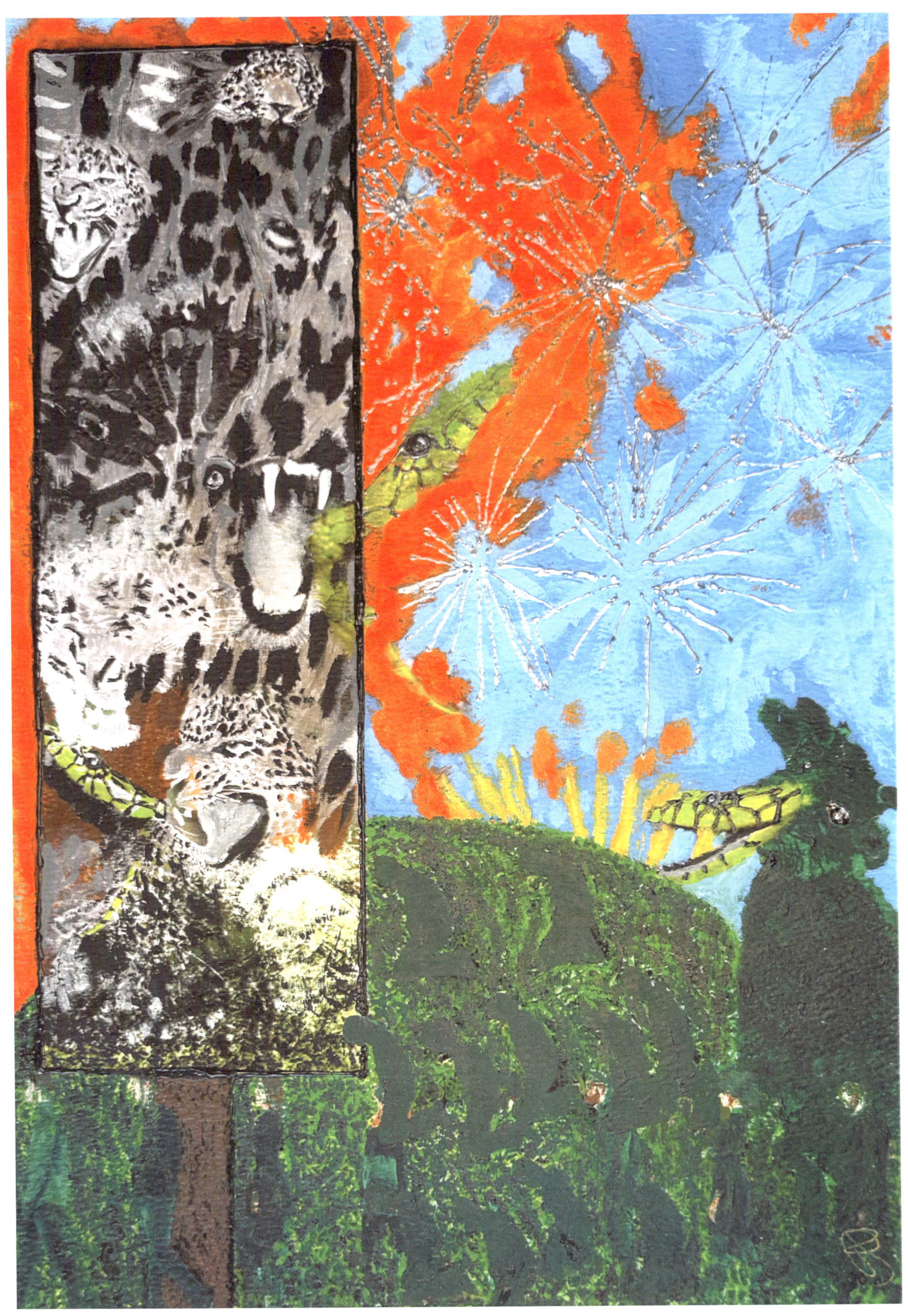

The Number of the Beast

The beast's mark appears to be a spiritual sign. John would have noted that these signs are reminiscent of the markings received by the Israelites when leaving Egypt, signifying how their changed status from slaves to "God's freed people" was to be reflected in their inner state of mind and outer actions.

All the same, there may be occasions when this "marking" becomes literal to indicate ownership or allegiance in an external way, and examples can be found throughout history.

In the Getty we see a literal example of people being marked.

In my painting I reference 666 as a prime example of visual exegesis when written in Greek, which John did. Visually the meaning presents itself almost immediately. Both Herder and Van der Waal noticed it!

"J. G. Herder noted that this sign resembles a mutilated Christ monogram, with a snake-like figure appearing between the Chi and Sigma. Of the many interpretations of 666, this one seems the most plausible. The biblical chokmah, or wisdom, can immediately recognise the caricature of the Messiah in this. We already saw that the dying and risen beast imitated Christ. Why should this mark not also be an imitatio Christi, slanderous and diabolical in nature and intent? The name-digit sign 'means' that a messiah-redeemer, a christ, is present, but the serpent is in the middle! We could also consider this to be a parody of the sign of Ezekiel 9.

13: [16]Also it causes all, both small and great, both rich and poor, both free and slave, to be marked on the right hand or the forehead, [17]so that no one can buy or sell who does not have the mark, that is, the name of the beast or the number of its name. [18]This calls for wisdom: let anyone with understanding calculate the number of the beast, for it is the number of a person. Its number is six hundred sixty-six.

"Redemption is approached from the demonic side. God's people want to be their own saviour! 666 does not extend to the number seven and indeed exhibits something imperfect and off-kilter. It is the number of complete imperfection and is the clearest indication that this devil's sign can never attain the perfection of 777."

I have painted the number on a British pound coin to emphasise the economic consequences of the sign.

The efforts by many scholars to work out the number through gematria seems to me out of place, for there is no need to apply that method anywhere else in Revelation or the rest of scripture in order to understand its meaning. And even when using it in this case, it yields no clear solution for who is referred to: there are too many possible candidates that quality.

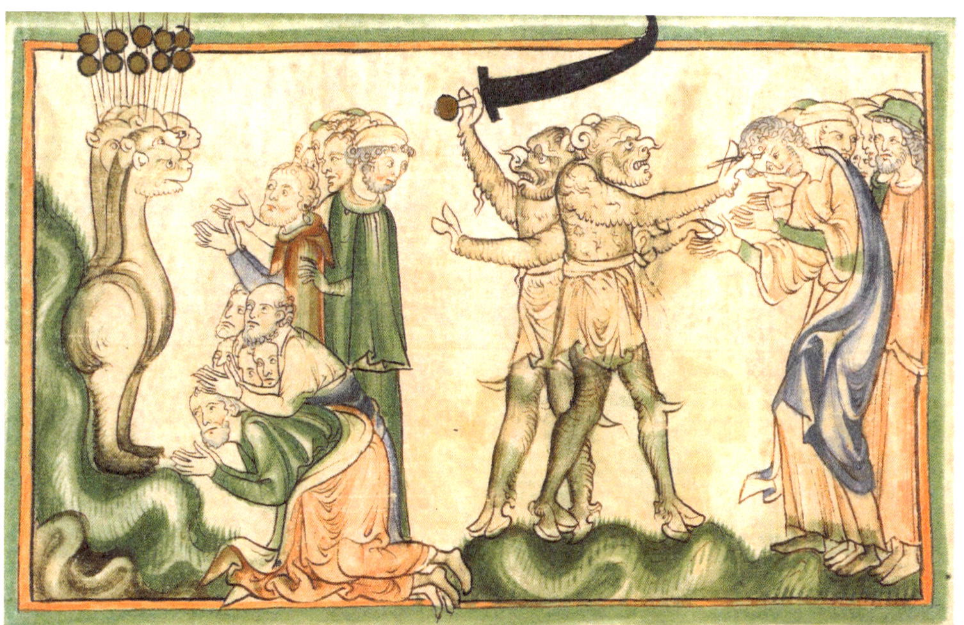

Although the number of the beast's mark is easily one of the most controversial passages in Revelation, 666 features only once in the Book. What is perhaps most interesting to reflect on is how that highlights our ability to major on minors!

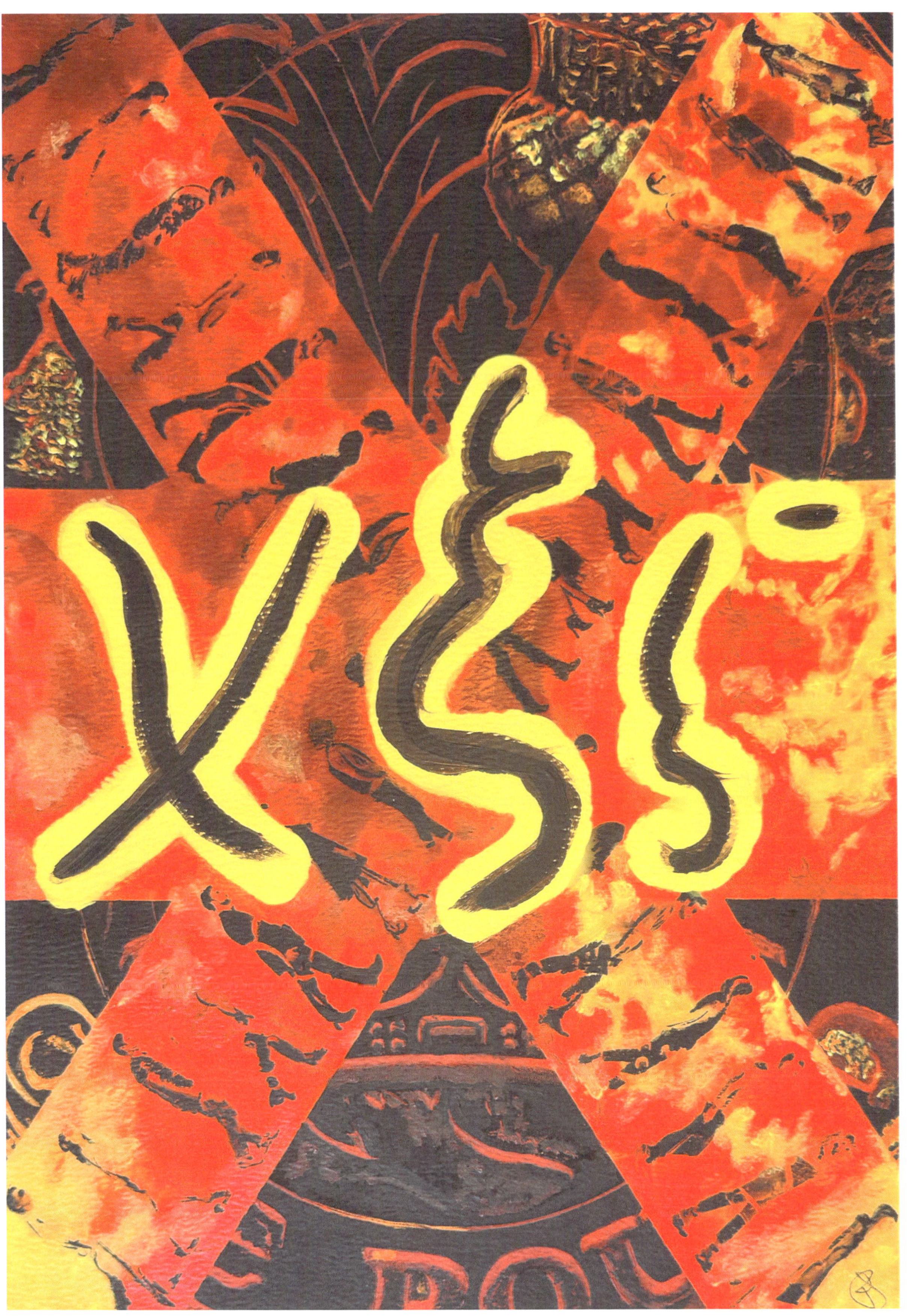

Liturgy of the Lamb

Significantly, immediately after the mark of the beast we are reminded of the mark of God the Father, written on the foreheads of the conquerors. And we are reminded again of the 144,000 standing with the Lamb on Mount Zion. In 7:7, they were numbered and set apart; here, they are described as spiritual virgins who follow the Lamb wherever he goes.

14: [1]Then I looked, and there was the Lamb, standing on Mount Zion! And with him were one hundred forty-four thousand who had his name and his Father's name written on their foreheads ...
[4]It is these who have not defiled themselves with women, for they are virgins; these follow the Lamb wherever he goes. They have been redeemed from humankind as first fruits for God and the Lamb, [5]and in their mouth no lie was found; they are blameless.

But who are the 144,000? Much has been written about them, and I will leave you to research that. To me, it is significant that they have been redeemed; they are, in fact, the first fruits for God and the Lamb, mentioned here in anticipation of the wheat harvest at the end of Revelation 14. Unlike the beasts and their followers, they are truthful and blameless.

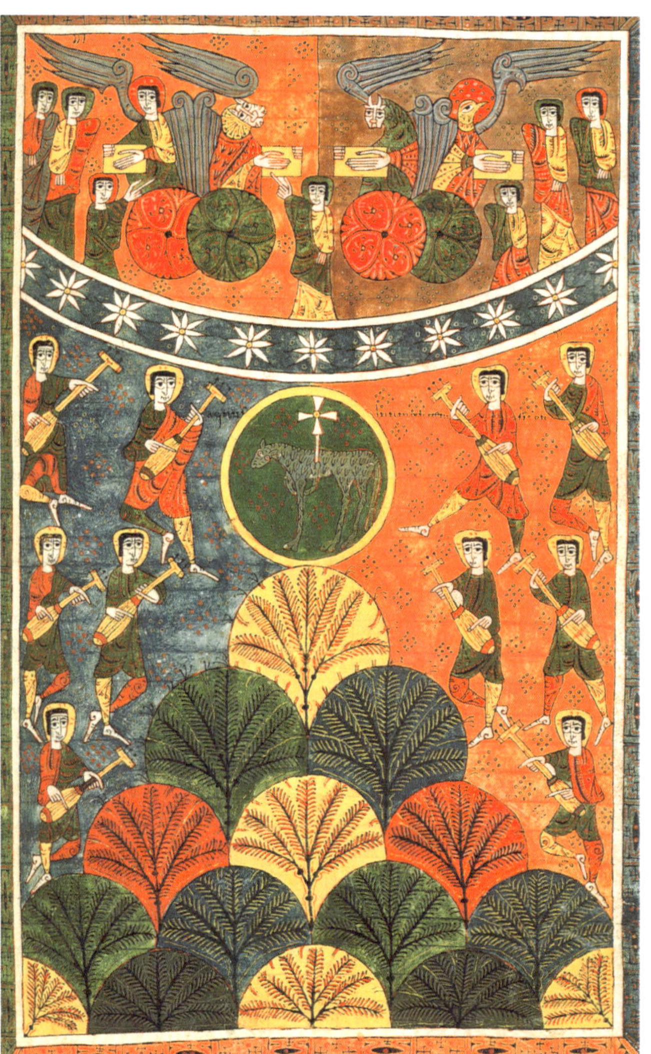

Whether they are martyrs, as some suggest, or whether they represent the first fruits in a more general sense, they are celebrating! I find it difficult to see them as representing all of God's people, nor am I convinced that this is a vision of the Parousia.

The image from the Silos is a joyful and colourful painting. It is easily explained and easy to "read", and it is a joy to contemplate: heaven and earth touch each other in the Lamb. The next verses are also included, referring to the new song, and the heavenly throne and entourage.

In my own painting I have returned to the familiar way I have been portraying the Lamb and the people. As in Revelation 7 I have again used a golden grid for suggesting the 144,000. But this time it is applied to the whole painting to create a very colourful whole. The grid also generates an air of mystery: it is difficult to see through it, much like looking through a crowd of 144,000; and who are the redeemed people? My entire painting is set in heaven.

Due to the reference to "virgins", some commentators see a military metaphor here, but I am not fully convinced. It seems to be written in direct contrast to the previous chapter and possibly depicts those in heaven who have died as a result of the beast's attacks.

While most commentators view this as a proleptic event, I see it as a group of people who have existed and continue to grow daily as those who die in the Lord are added, as we will see later in Revelation 14. They are the first fruits of the final harvest.

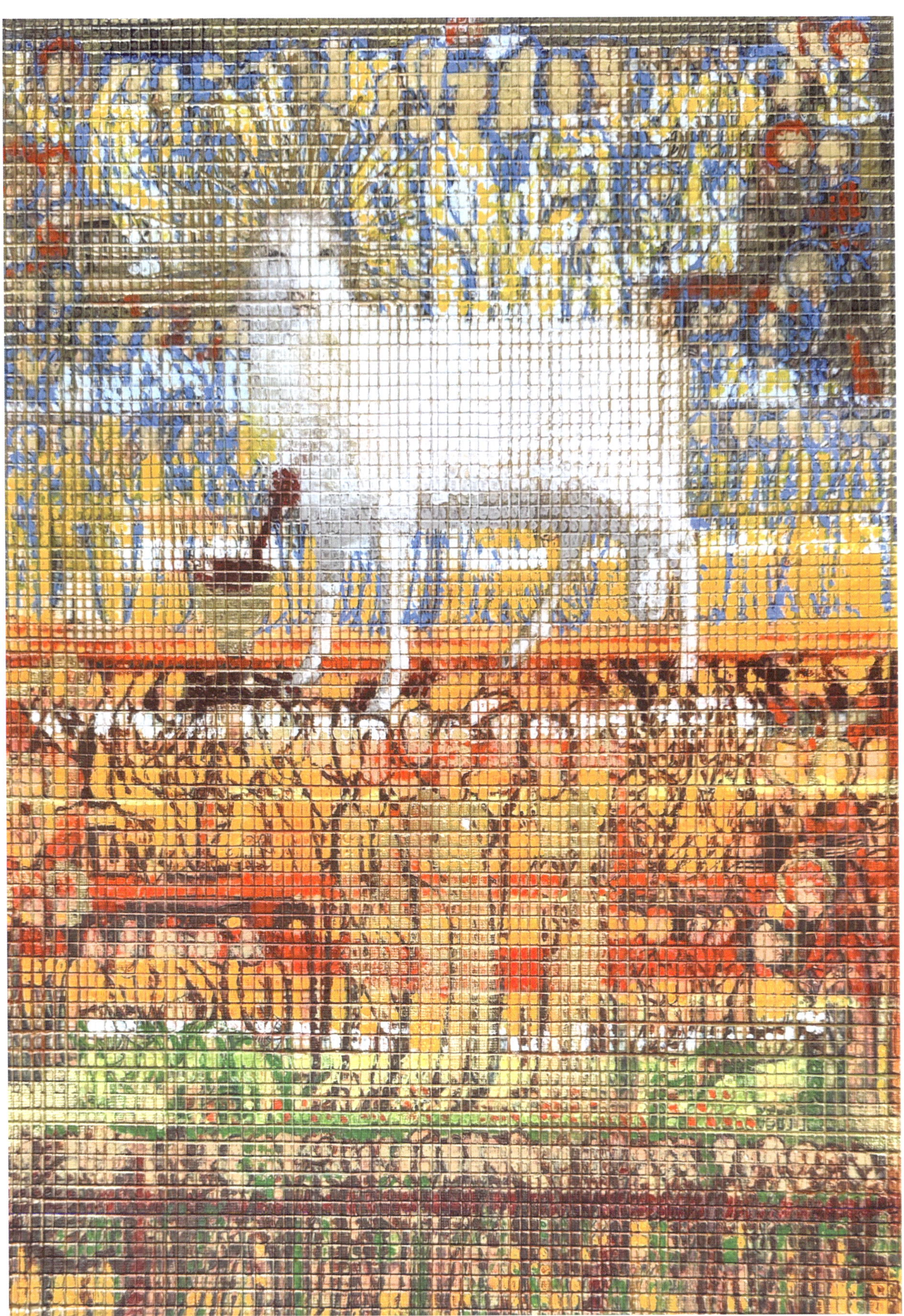

A New Song to Learn

John usually sees a lot, but this time he hears it. And, what a sound! Loud and harmonious. It's not immediately clear who is singing, but I guess it must be the 144,000 who are learning this new song. For this is a song that can only be learnt by the redeemed. Perhaps it is a deeply personal testimony of victory by those who lived by faith? Those who did not live faithfully cannot express that? In any case, it suggests this song must be based on the experience of having lived by faith.

> *14: 2And I heard a voice from heaven like the sound of many waters and like the sound of loud thunder; the voice I heard was like the sound of harpists playing on their harps, 3and they sing a new song before the throne and before the four living creatures and before the elders. No one could learn that song except the one hundred forty-four thousand who have been redeemed from the earth.*

I just love the way Getty makes John having to kneel down in order to listen to this, thereby unwittingly "joining" the worshippers? I also love the way the creatures are using hymnals to sing.

In my own painting, I once more have used the grid of the 144,000 and painted the throne of God surrounded by the rainbow and the living creatures. I also painted seven harps (though that number is not specified in the text) to produce the swirling music inside the many waters.

But why a "new" song? This heavenly song is "new" because it is the expression of their seeing the Lamb. It is not the "old" laments and songs of encouragement they sang on the way. It is the new song they sing when they see reality, as opposed to what they sang about when they longed for it. It is impossible to learn this song without the experience. It appears to be a song that is activated when God's servants finally see the throne of God. This song appears to be perfect, true, beautiful and majestic.

This song is worship at its very best, with no distractions from sin, no other allegiances, only joy and thankfulness in the presence of God, using all the musicality our hearts have been given: the sound of God's life, the sound of many waters.

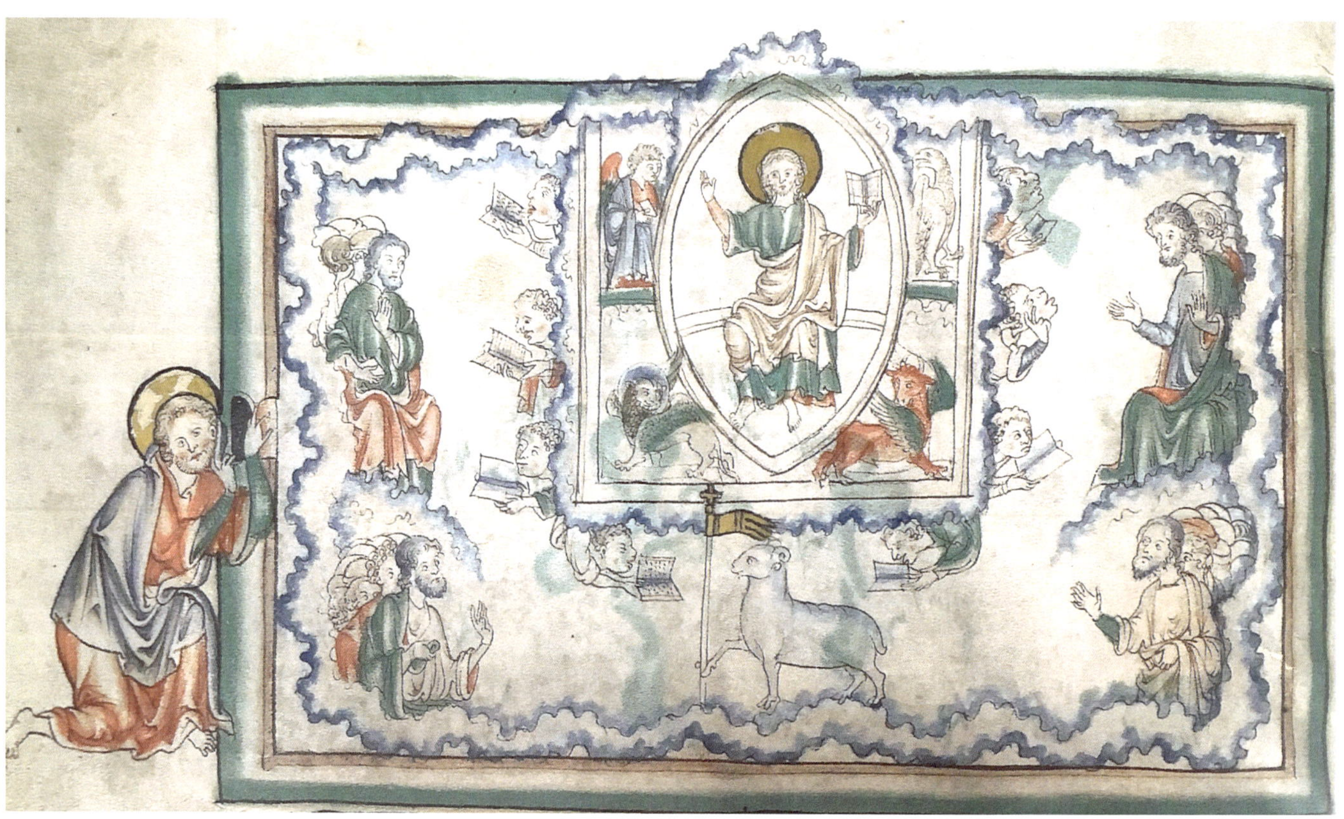

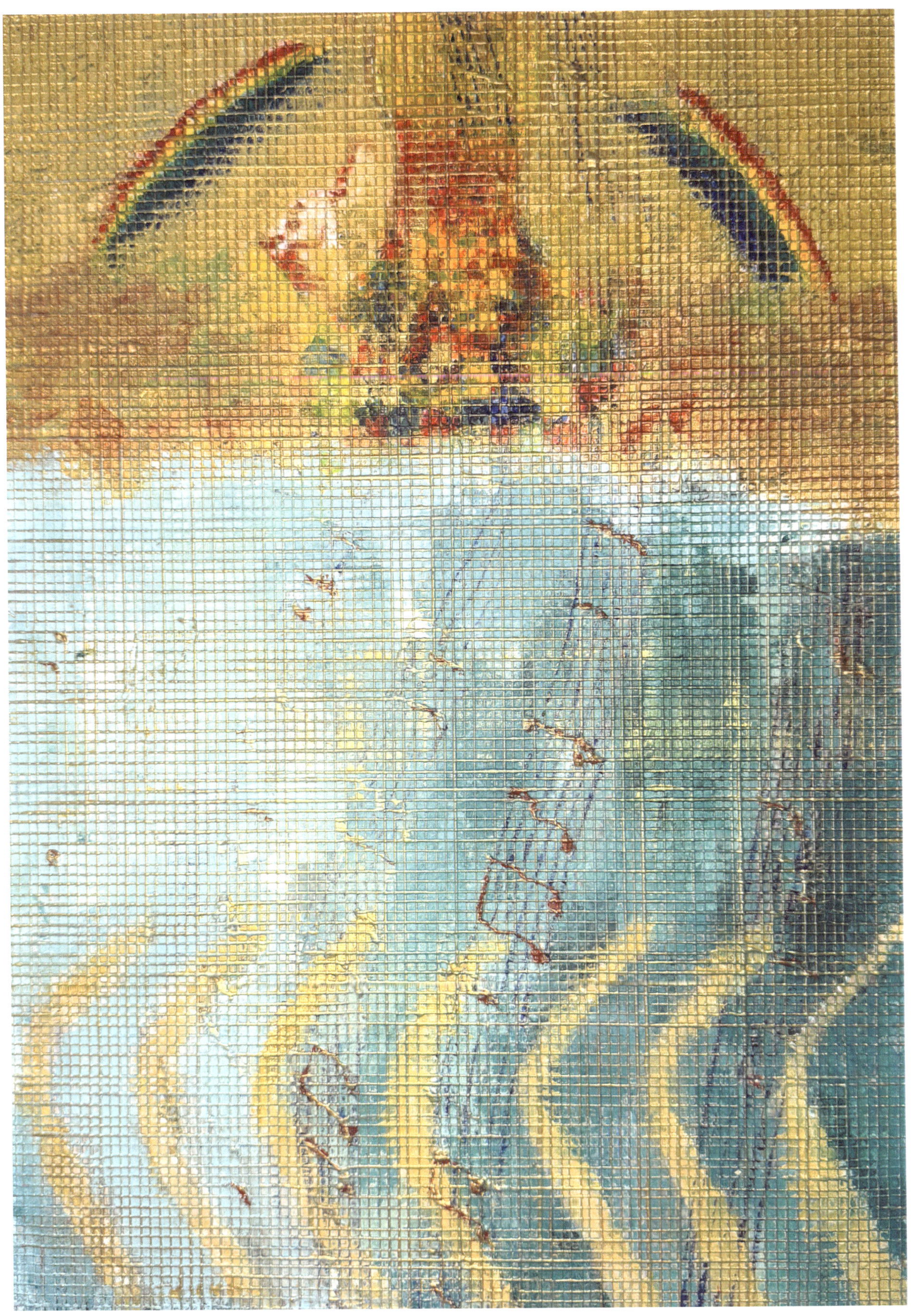

The Eternal Gospel

> *14: [6]Then I saw another angel flying in midheaven, with an eternal gospel to proclaim to those who live on the earth – to every nation and tribe and language and people. [7]He said in a loud voice, "Fear God and give him glory, for the hour of his judgment has come, and worship him who made heaven and earth, the sea and the springs of water."...*
>
> *14: [12]This calls for patient endurance on the part of the people of God who keep his commands and remain faithful to Jesus.*

There is some debate as to which angel it refers to when it says "another" angel. Does it refer to the angel of the last trumpet, or possibly the great angel standing on the sea and the earth in Revelation 10? The good news or "eternal gospel" here appears as a noun; in Revelation 10:6, the verb form is used for the "announcing" to the prophets in the past. That indicates a clear connection between this message and the message of the great angel. Along with many commentators, I think the revelation of how the mystery of God will be fulfilled is what is encapsulated in the meaning of the whole of Revelation 12–22.

This eternal gospel is for the whole world: every nation, tribe, language and people. It is the gospel that resonates from the Old into the New Testament, and continues to resonate today and into the future; it is eternal.

The Val-Dieu uses a banner bearing the words to portray the message. Note that this is the only place in Revelation where angels appear to fly. The message is simple and easy to understand and not so easy to do: Fear God, give Him glory and worship Him alone; the hour of judgement has come.

I have coupled this message with the call for endurance to the saints, as it is primarily addressed to them. After this angel, another two will appear to proclaim the good news!

The next two visions are closely connected to this one, which is why I designed my three paintings on the messages of the three angels as a triptych.

In this first triptych painting, John sees the angel addressing the earth. I used my painting of the church in Philadelphia but could have portrayed any church. Some members of that church have been martyred, so she bears marks in red (for blood) and blue (for faith). I have used gold to show God on his throne, within the huge trumpet representing the loud voice.

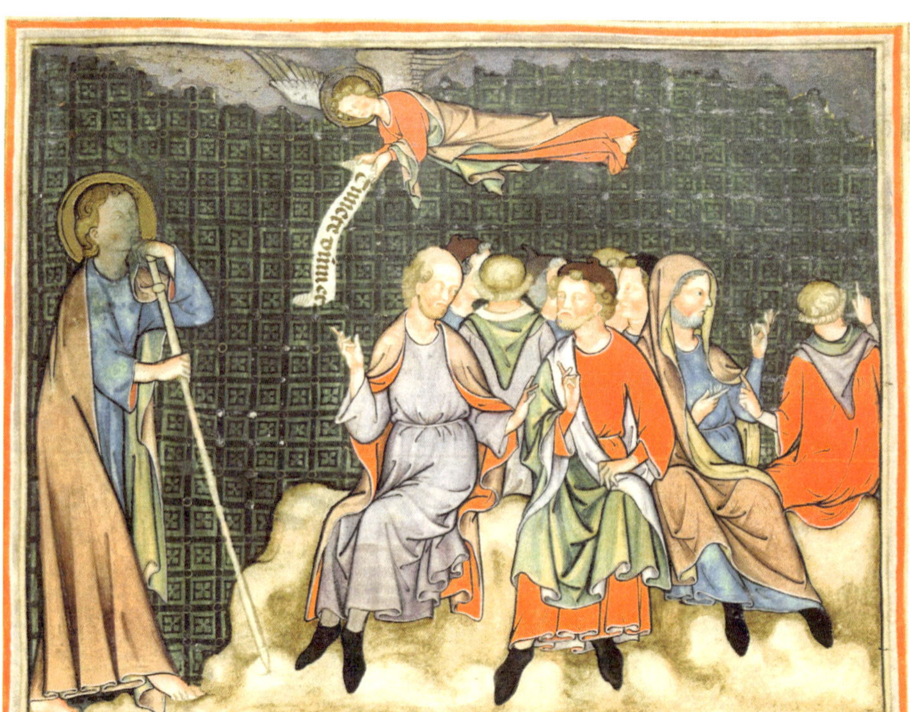

It is interesting that on Reformation Sunday every year, many churches still use this text and vision to commemorate the preaching of the Reformation, and particularly that of Luther. That is one particular application among many.

This is not judgement itself yet, but it is the announcement of imminent judgement. It acknowledges that this announcement will create fear in the hearers, but not with the goal of crippling them with fear, for it urges them to be ready to "give glory to God".

What is revealed in these announcements, is that judgement is part of the good news!

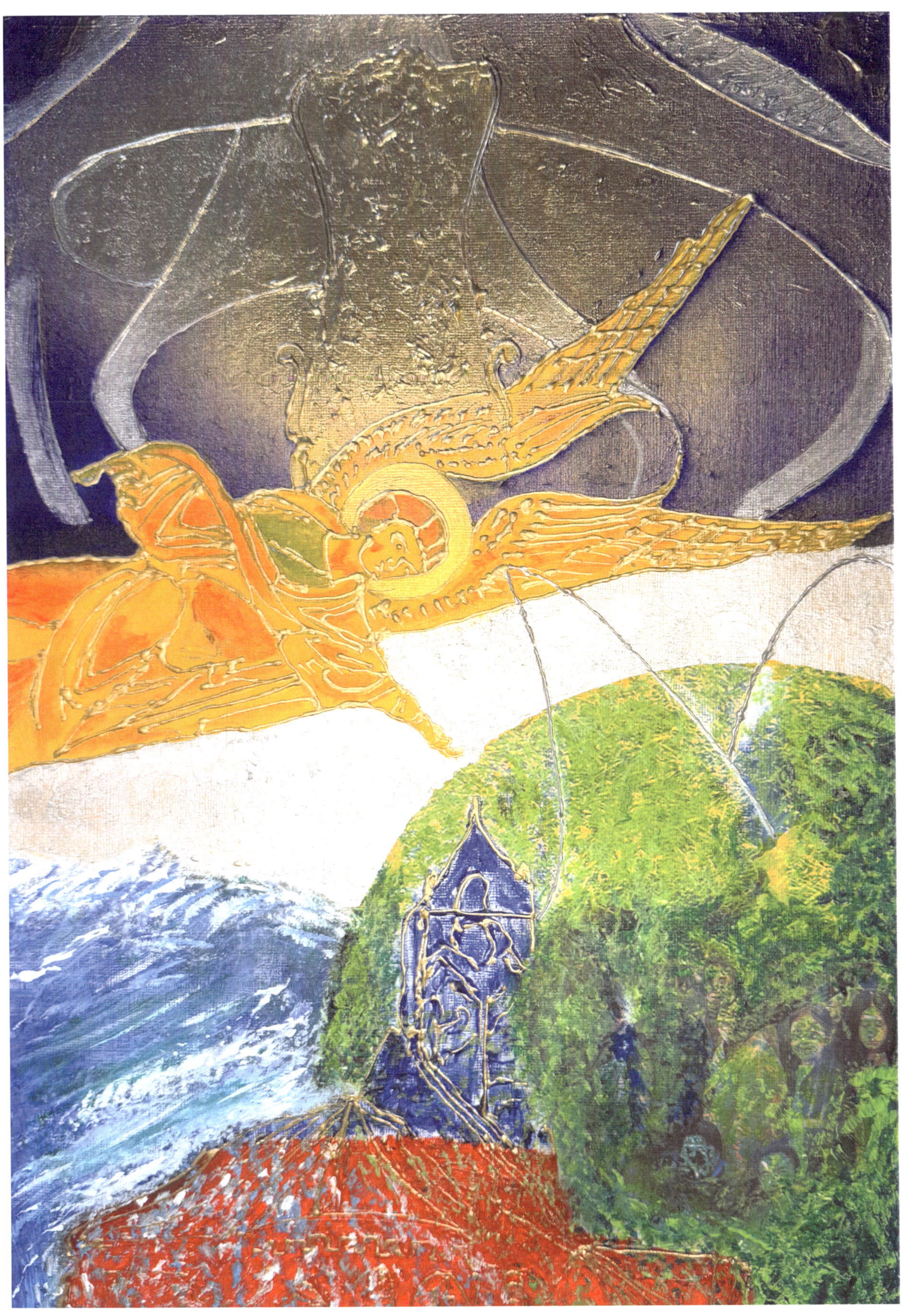

Fallen is Babylon

This is the second angel of my triptych, and another one announcing something to happen as if it had already happened: "Fallen, fallen is Babylon the great!"

This is the first time Babylon is mentioned in the visions. The OT nation of Israel and the surrounding nations had a long history of subjection to the Babylonian Empire. Babylon was a godless and proud city, ruled by the emperor and opposed to God. The city became a symbol of quintessential evil.

What is Babylon? Much has been written about what Babylon represents here. Some say it is the city of Jerusalem, while others identify it as Rome. And others view it as religious Rome, or the Roman Catholic Church. All such interpretations have merit in particular contexts, but none exhausts the meaning of "Babylon".

It is clearly a powerful city, set against God: the antithesis of the New Jerusalem. And it has worldwide influence. Its influence also reaches back to the very beginning of humanity, as well as forwards to the megacities of the world still to come.

14: [8]Then another angel, a second, followed, saying, "Fallen, fallen is Babylon the great! She has made all nations drink of the wine of the wrath of her prostitution."

The Val-Dieu painting below depicts it as one city: the city of the devil, composed of all the wicked, as stated by the Getty.

In my painting, I interpret this as another loud statement. I started by superimposing skylines of New York, Moscow, Beijing, Jerusalem, Rome, Babylon and Manchester, showing them in the process of being destroyed. As the painting developed, it became increasingly abstract, set in a red sea of destruction signifying God's wrath. But it is not uncontrolled destruction. I show God clearly present, in the gold.

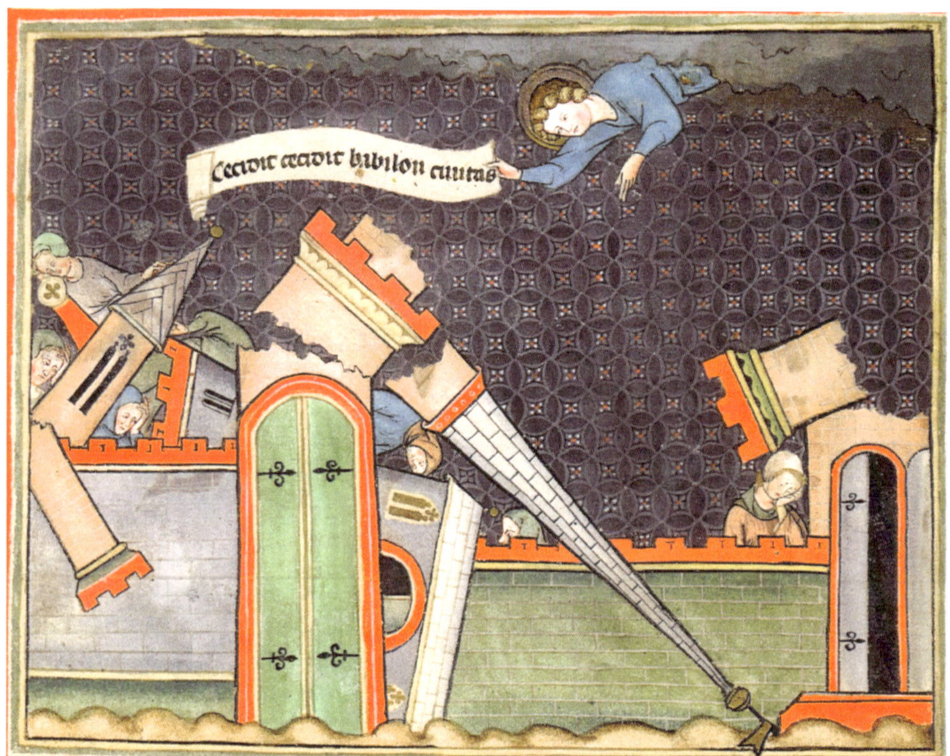

Of course, many of the cities mentioned above have long histories. Rome has not been destroyed completely. This causes problems for those who interpret the Bible literally. I believe these cities have to be interpreted spiritually, as realms where the beasts have their sway. Such cities, and all those not named, are real today.

In the present, the churches must endure their presence by holding to God's commandments. They are encouraged to resist drinking the wine or participating in the prostitution of the nations. For the angel assures them: "Fallen, fallen is Babylon the great."

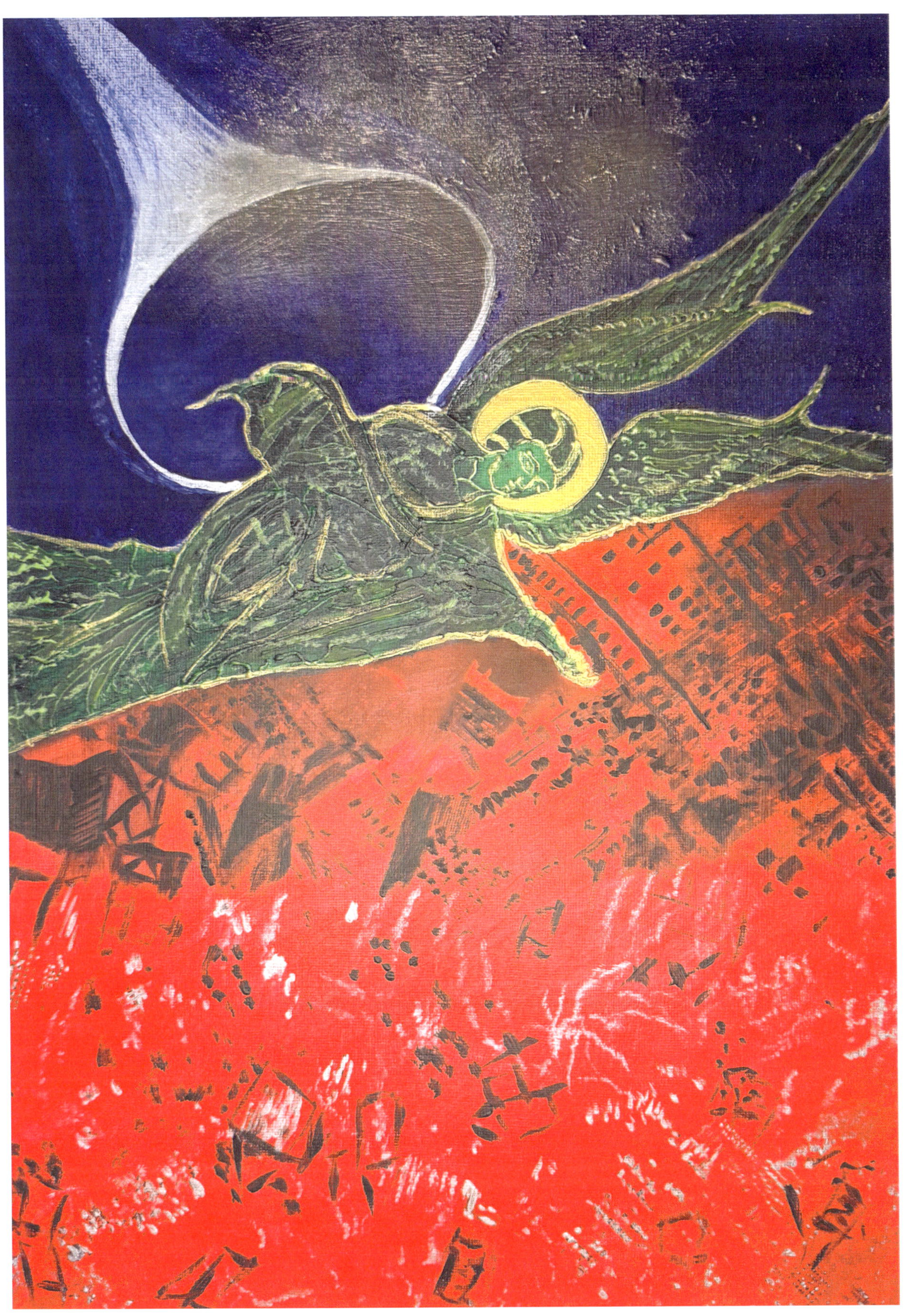

God's Judgement Revealed

The third announcement informs the churches of what will happen to the followers of the beast who have been marked with his number. Together with the beast, they will drink undiluted wine and be tormented with fire and sulphur. The smoke of their torment will rise forever. Those who worship the beast, his image, or receive his mark will have no rest day or night.

John knows that the churches should take this message very seriously. It is a call for them to endure, not to fall for the evil beast and not to follow him, no matter how many miracles he performs.

Did John experience this as a description of the final punishment of all the followers of the beast? Boring argues that doctrinal conclusions should not be based on this kind of "poetic" text, which we should read figuratively. Those who believe that this is a proleptic statement argue that it describes the fate of unbelievers in eternity. Still others say it is a temporary judgement inflicted by the devil himself, and witnessed by the Lamb and the holy angels. Caird and Paul, for example, believe this passage should be read as describing the final destruction of the followers of the beast, with the fire consuming them completely, whereas Ellul distinguishes between judgement and condemnation and argues that this punishment will only last until the new heaven and new earth are created. Clearly, there are still many chapters before we get to the end of Revelation.

14: [9]Then another angel, a third, followed them, crying with a loud voice, "Those who worship the beast and its image and receive the brand on their foreheads or on their hands, [10]they will also drink the wine of God's wrath, poured unmixed into the cup of his anger, and they will be tormented with fire and sulfur in the presence of the holy angels and in the presence of the Lamb. [11]And the smoke of their torment goes up forever and ever. There is no rest day or night for those who worship the beast and its image and for anyone who receives the brand of its name."

Interestingly, while images of unbelievers being thrown into everlasting fires and hell were popular in the Middle Ages, Getty does not depict that here. Perhaps because John does not here appear to describe visions of destruction that he saw; he records what he heard the angels announce!

In my own painting, I reflected on the presence of the holy angels and the Lamb. With each angel, I included in the background an expression of the content of the message they announce.

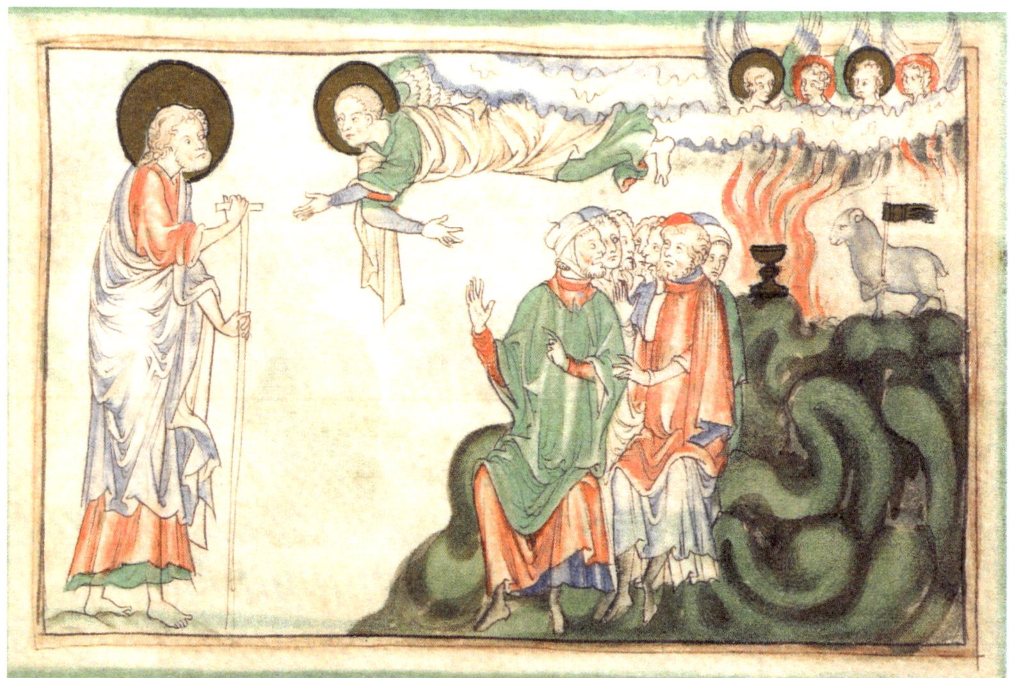

The rising smoke I portrayed in this announcement is a familiar symbol for destruction, usually related to Sodom and Gomorrah. But it is not clear that John "saw" exactly this; we know he heard it.

Is this torment self-inflicted, as Tonstad has suggested, or does it come from God himself? Does He allow this torment, or is He the author of it? The text does not address such specific questions. John's response was to urge the churches to persevere: there will be no rest for those who follow the beasts!

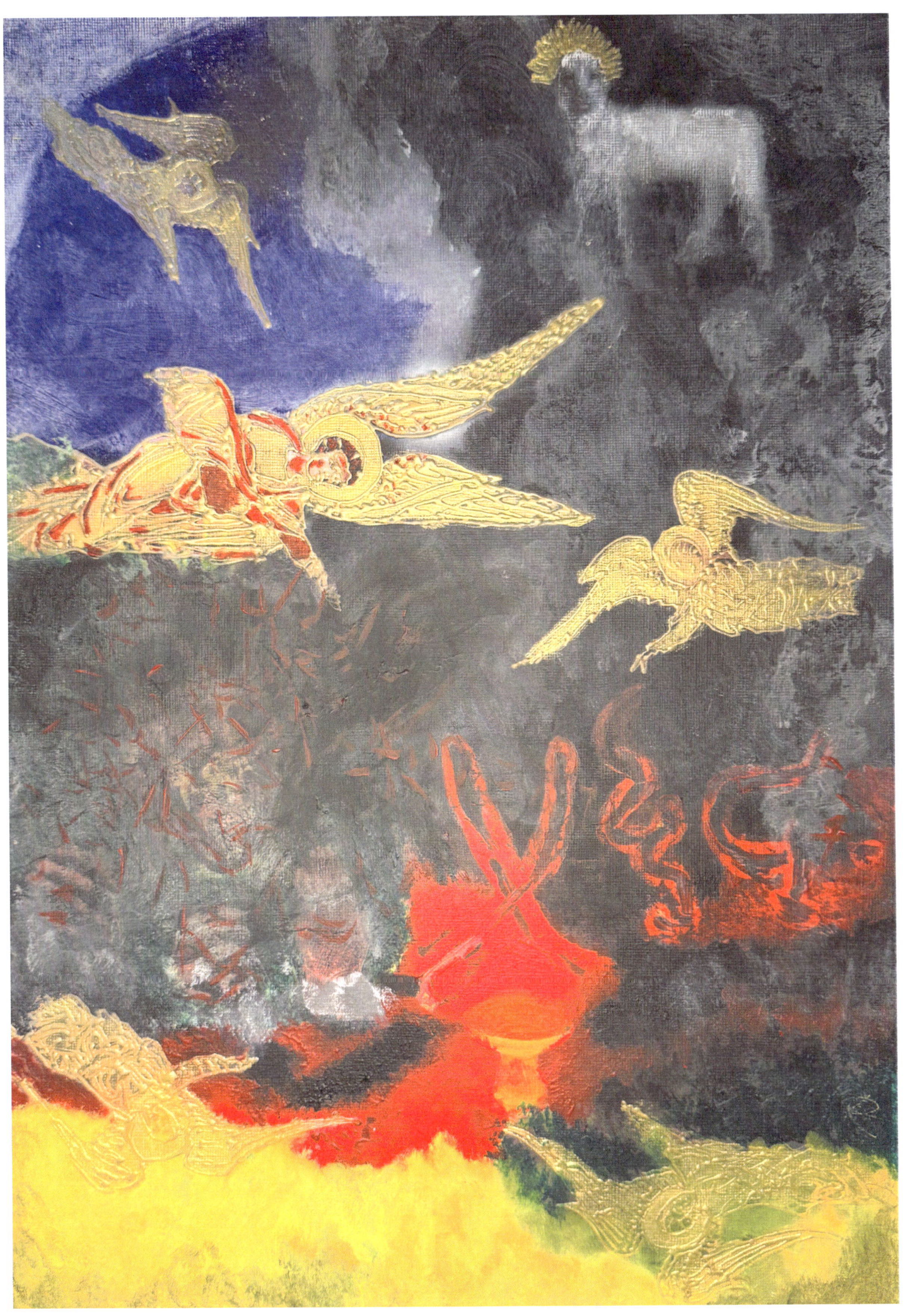

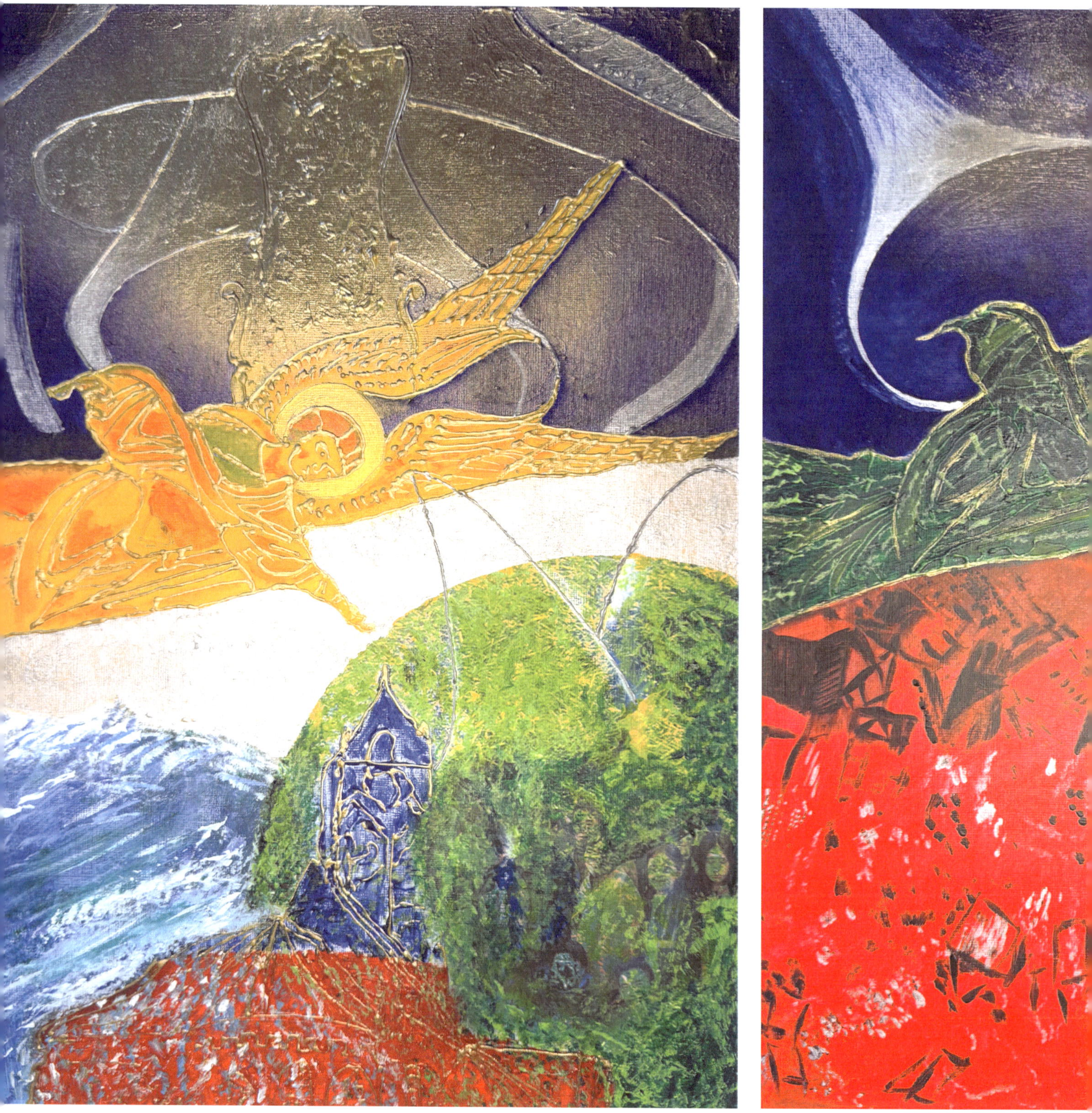

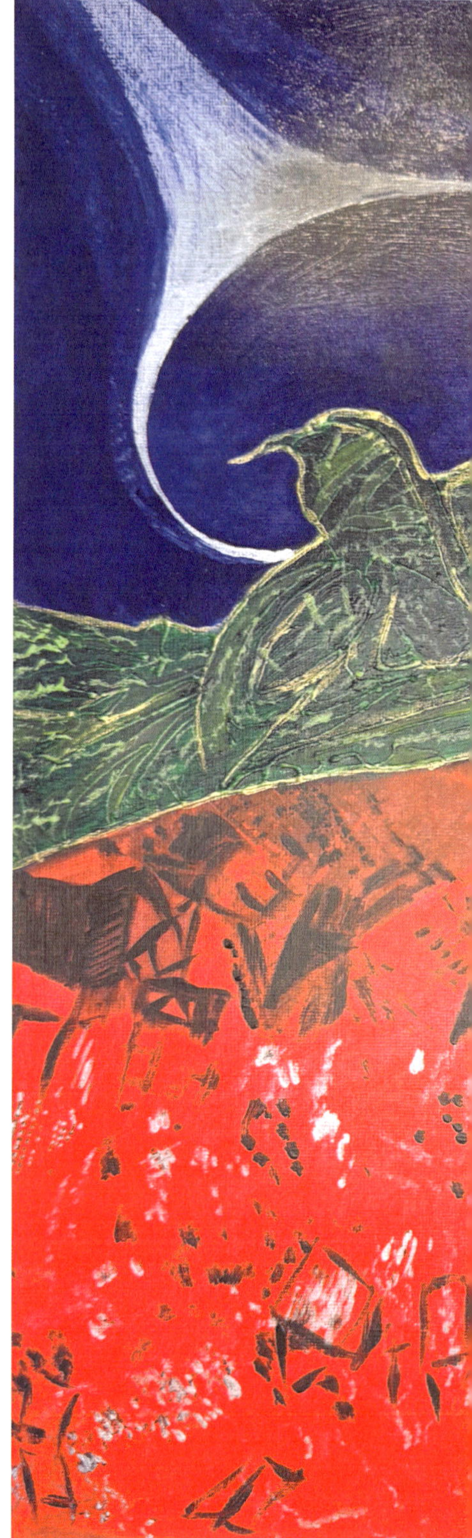

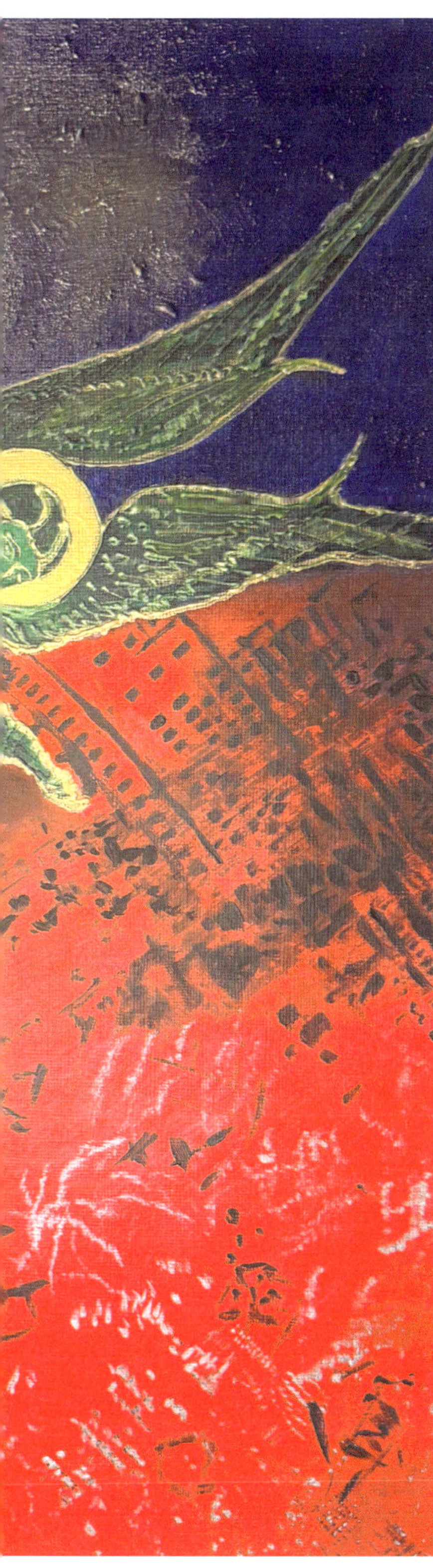

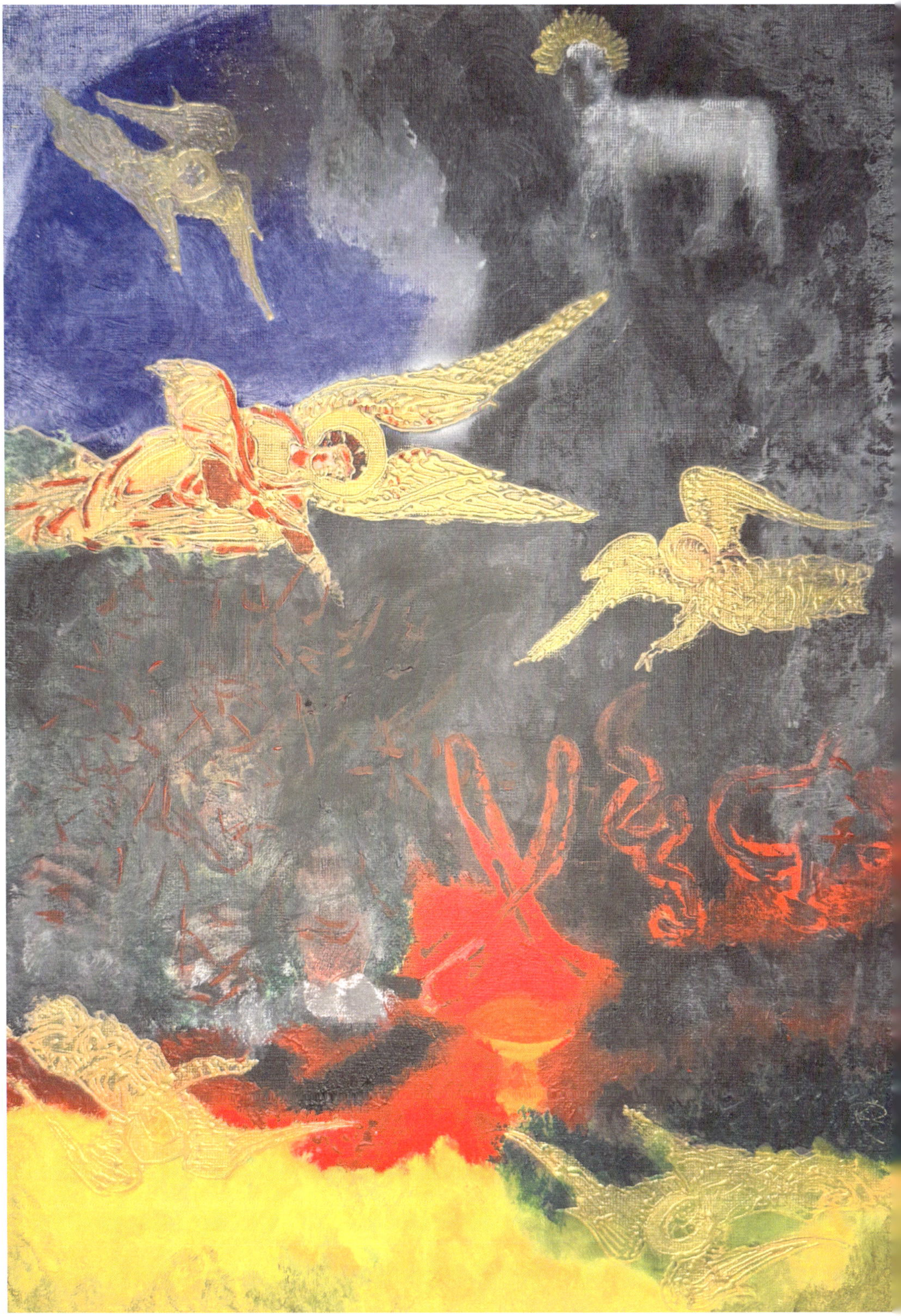

Endurance and Blessedness

Finally, we understand why the three angels delivered their messages of destruction, which appear to have taken place while, in the cases of Babylon and Rome, for example, the events had yet to occur. They did so to encourage the Church to prepare more urgently for the battle to keep God's commandments and hold fast to their faith in Him against all odds. The good news was the devastating judgement of the beasts and their followers, as well as the civil orders they established. Although the beasts' authority may seem overwhelming at first, the churches were assured that justice would ultimately prevail against these powers.

14: [12]Here is a call for the endurance of the saints, those who keep the commandments of God and hold fast to the faith of Jesus. [13]And I heard a voice from heaven saying, "Write this: Blessed are the dead who from now on die in the Lord." "Yes," says the Spirit, "they will rest from their labors, for their deeds follow them.

At this point, the Spirit inspires John to insert the next beatitude: "Blessed are the dead who from now on die in the Lord."

Some early commentators, in answering the question how the dead could die again, suggested that first believers need to die to themselves, and then they die in the Lord. I rather like that.

This verse is often used at funeral services and is generally seen as a statement about the death of all believers. But in this context, "from now on", I believe it most likely applies to those who died as martyrs in the beasts' attacks whose martyrdom becomes the means for conquering the beasts. What is revealed, and the satanic forces may not have envisaged is that the deaths of the martyrs are so highly regarded, remembered and rewarded by God.

The Val-Dieu provides a delightful image of all this. It is so good; I have quoted it just as many other illustrators have done.

In the lower half of my painting, I removed two people from the Val-Dieu, which depicts seven, but I still maintain the "perfect" number in the heavenly part above.

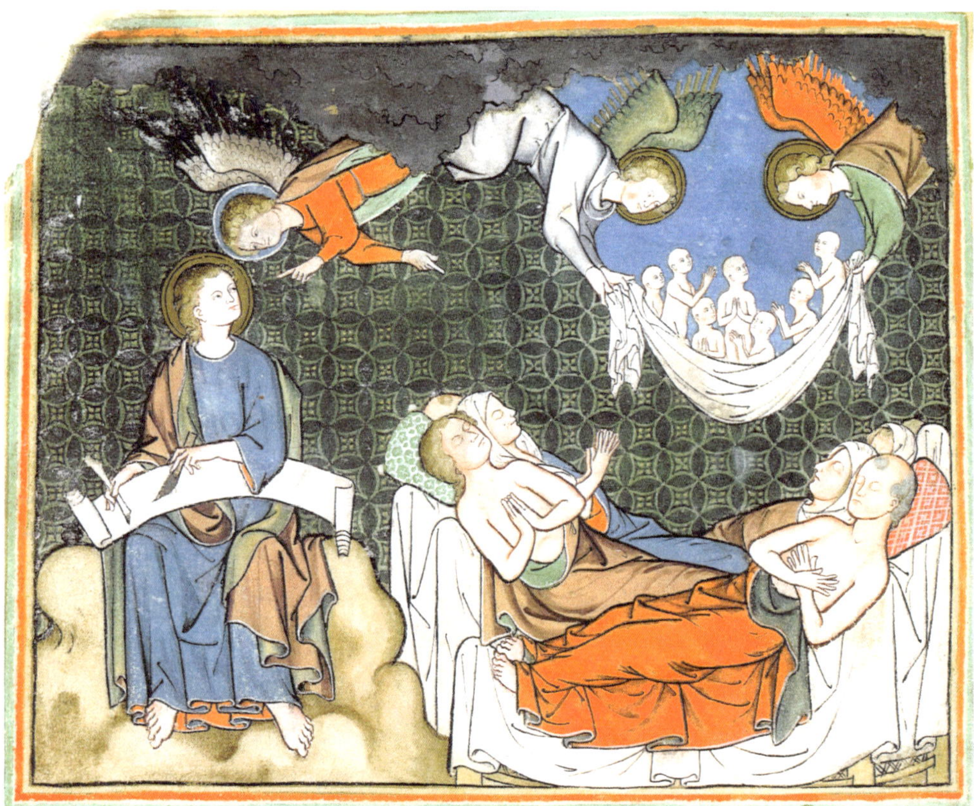

And I added the church in the centre, because I think these verses are directed both to the church and to individual members. I love the way the martyrs are lifted up and prepared to come down on the last day, like the heavenly Jerusalem, as the bride of Christ.

The revelation does not continue to dwell on the beasts or their followers. Instead, John encourages the churches to meditate on the message of hope that follows. In Revelation 13 and 14 the most important call to the churches is to endure, endure, endure. Despite the apparent power of the beasts, it is not in vain. It is being seen and will be remembered and rewarded into eternity.

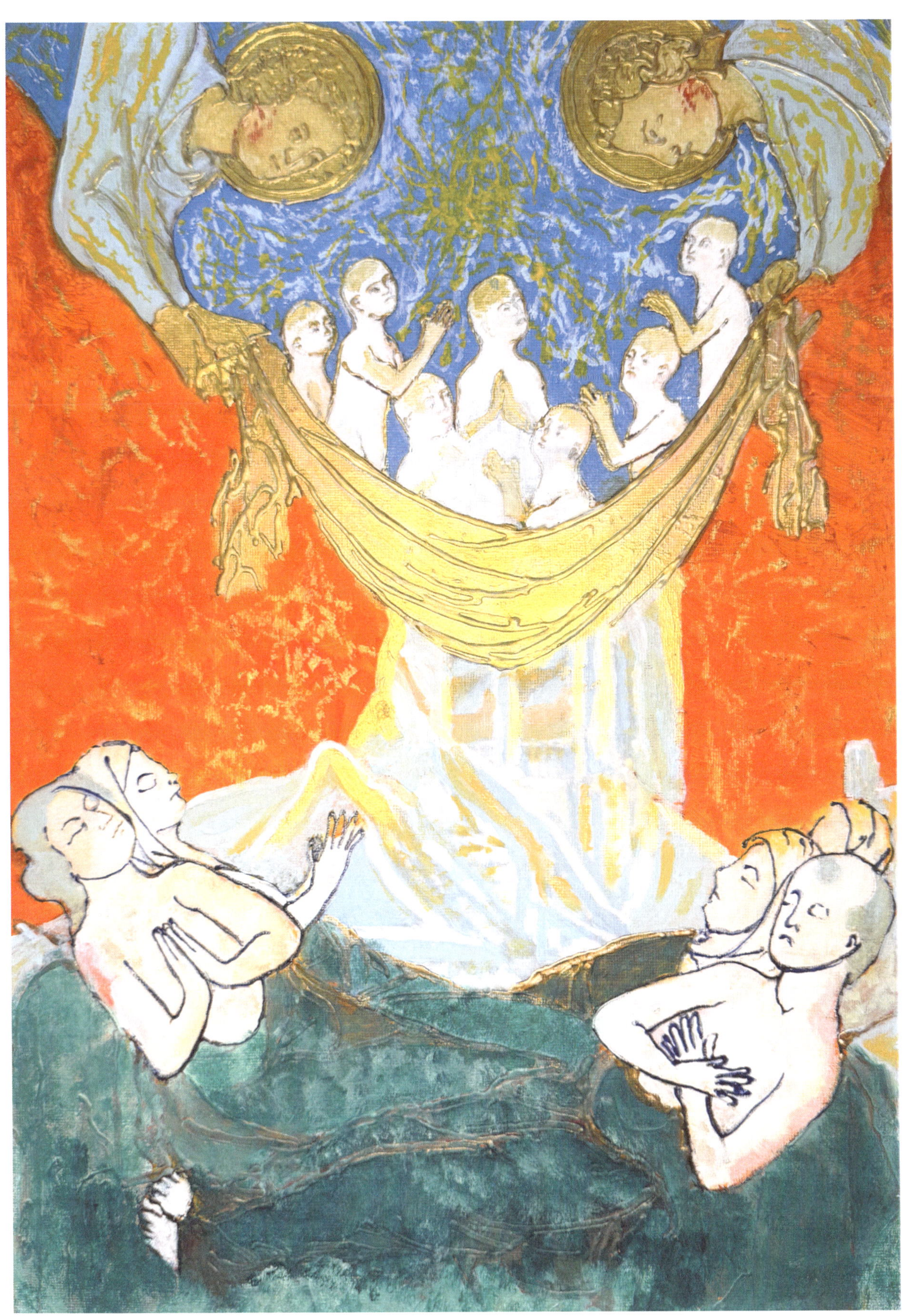

Like a Son of Man

Next John sees a white cloud and someone seated on it, like the Son of Man and wearing a golden crown and holding a sharp sickle in his hand.

> *14: 14 Then I looked, and there was a white cloud, and*
> *seated on the cloud was one like the Son of Man, with*
> *a golden crown on his head and a sharp sickle in his*
> *hand! 15 Another angel came out of the temple, calling*
> *with a loud voice to the one who sat on the cloud, "Use*
> *your sickle and reap, for the hour to reap has come,*
> *because the harvest of the earth is fully ripe." 16 So the*
> *one who sat on the cloud swung his sickle over the*
> *earth, and the earth was reaped.*

Who is the Son of Man? Some say he is another angel, to make seven angel appearances in total in this biblical chapter. However, it is a clear reference to the early visions in 1:7 and 1:13 where the Son of Man also appears. The name is quoted from Daniel 7, and all four Gospel writers record Jesus applying it to himself. It is not problematic when another angel who emerges from the temple, commands the Son of Man and he obeys! The angel in this case is clearly the mouthpiece of God Himself. And I personally find it refreshing to reflect on what John hears and sees here, and records: a humble, serving Son of Man!

The Morgan Beatus depicts the Son of Man, which is a title for Christ, as an angel with wings who sits on a golden cloud. Further, the painting depicts both harvests as allegorical representations of the last judgement.

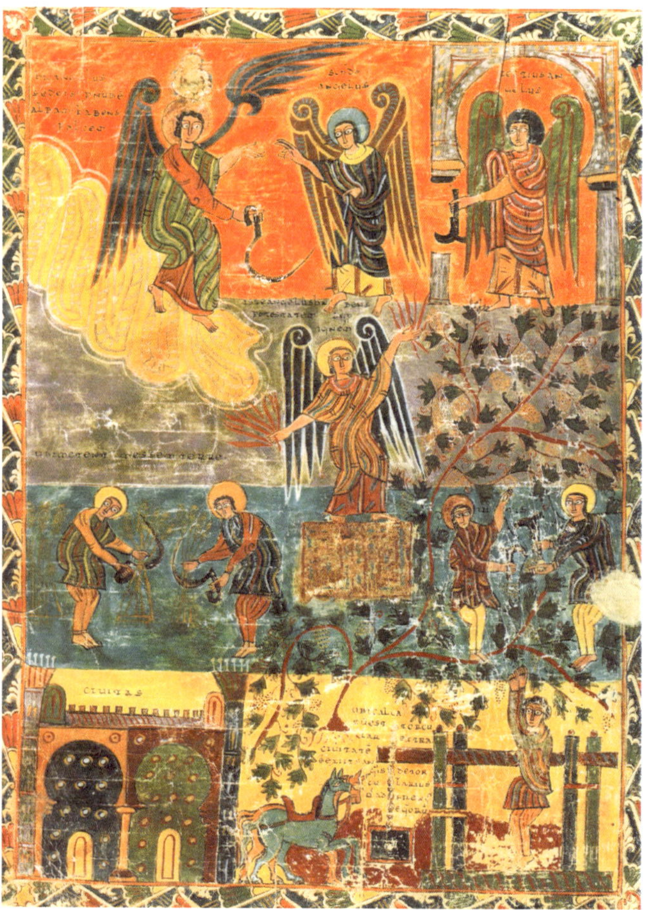

In my own painting, I portray the grain harvest as the harvest of believers, hence the gold and sheaves with figure-like shapes. The corn kernels are in gold. The cloud dominates the scene in the shape of a number 8. Christ's head, which I placed in the cloud, refers to Story 4, and His hand with the sickle is seen lower down in the painting. The angel emerging from the heavenly temple, which signifies the presence of God, speaks in through a golden trumpet, which signifies a loud voice: "Use your sickle and reap."

This vision gives John a foretaste of what will happen in response to the church's endurance and faith in God. By giving the Son of Man the same crown as for the Lamb in Story 67, I connect them visually. There, the Lamb of God celebrates the first fruits; here, the rest of the harvest is gathered in, possibly previewing the two resurrections that Revelation 20 will tell us about.

But this harvest is mentioned here already to reveal Jesus and what He has done. Some scholars interpret this harvest and the next one as referring to the bread and wine of the Eucharist, or the Lord's Supper. I will return to that idea in the two next paintings.

The spiritual harvest has been collected, and it is a golden wonder! In my painting I tried to capture visually the comfort this gave John, and hopefully would give the churches who will receive his writing, after the dark revelation of the frightful beasts and their work, their followers and their successes. I wonder if John was relieved to record this vision referring to Jesus, the slain Lamb, shown in receipt of His whole harvest.

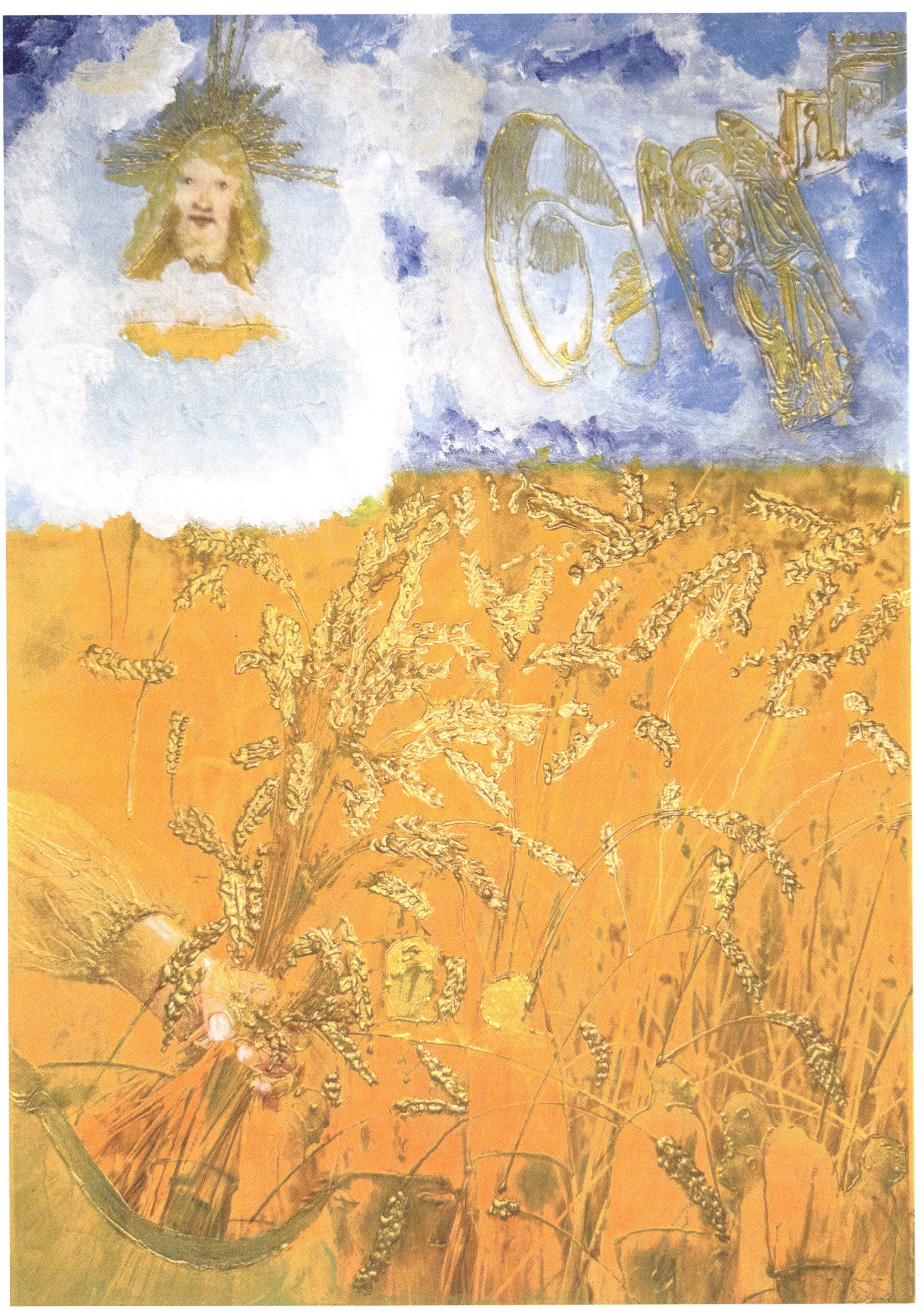

The Vintage

There is another angel emerging from the temple with a sharp sickle, and another angel from the altar.

Dietsche treats us to the whole chapter again below. Take your time to look at this painting, as he presents all the details clearly and wonderfully. The harvest in this story is just above the bottom right-hand corner.

Looking at both paintings, I was very pleased that I had come up with a similar colour scheme!

In my painting, the temple and the altar are in the top corners, with the respective angels emerging from them. The grapes on the vine are full and ripe. For clarity and diversity, I added white grapes, even though the text only mentions one vine.

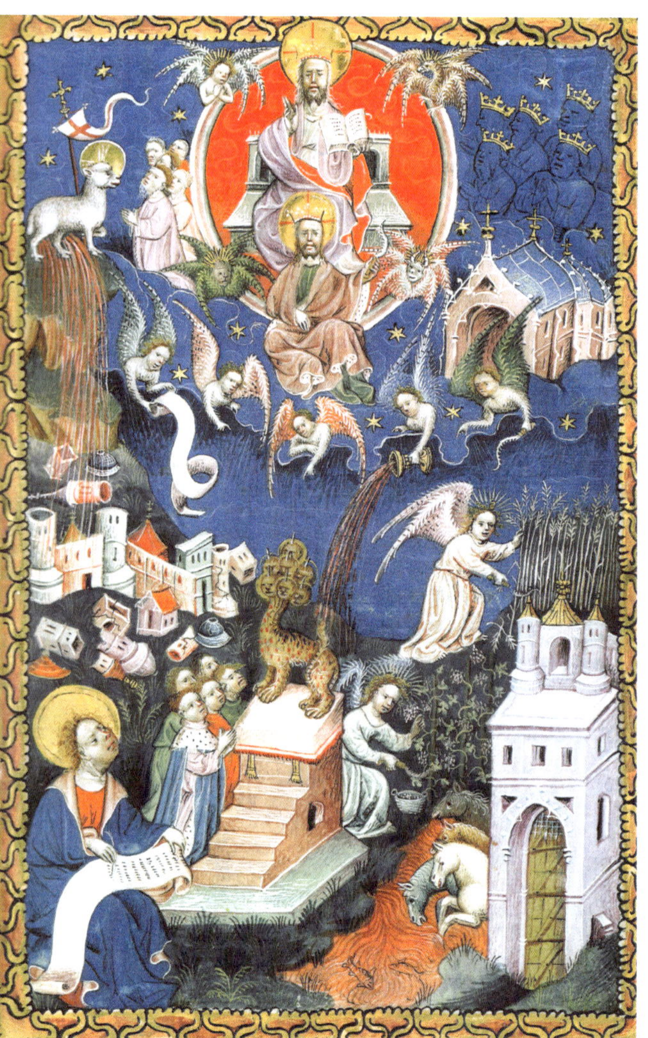

14: [17]Then another angel came out of the temple in heaven, and he, too, had a sharp sickle. [18]Then another angel came out from the altar, the angel who has authority over fire, and he called with a loud voice to him who had the sharp sickle, "Use your sharp sickle and gather the clusters of the vine of the earth, for its grapes are ripe." [19]So the angel swung his sickle over the earth and gathered the vintage of the earth, and he threw it into the great winepress of the wrath of God.

The feet below represent the treading of grapes in the great winepress of God's wrath. We are told that the trodden grapes release blood, which I will revisit in the next Story.

What does this harvest represent? This appears to refer to a harvest of the wicked, with both God's wrath and blood being mentioned, and many commentators agree on this. [I hope to add more to this in the next Story.]

But Caird and Leithart take a different view. They see this as a reference that indicates the vintages of the redeemed and of the wicked, and they present plausible arguments, though, to my mind, the text neither states nor implies it. And, Leithart does make a valuable observation that is not found in other commentaries: that there is talk here of only one vine. Leithart identifies that vine as symbolic of Israel. He then sees this harvest primarily in terms of the people of God of the Old Covenant, both in a positive and a negative light. I find that plausible, and it would allow for judgement on God's own people to happen first.

While the one vine can be identified with Israel, it can also be identified with Jesus Himself. Seeing that He is the author and subject of Revelation, it would make sense that this also is a reference to His sacrifice.

The next Story will help us to make that association even more strongly. The presence of temple and altar here affirm such an association.

What does this harvest signify? I agree with those who see here, first, Christ taking the wrath of God on behalf of those harvested in the grain harvest. And, secondly, with those who see in this God's wrath on those who reject Christ's friendship and refuse to worship Him as King.

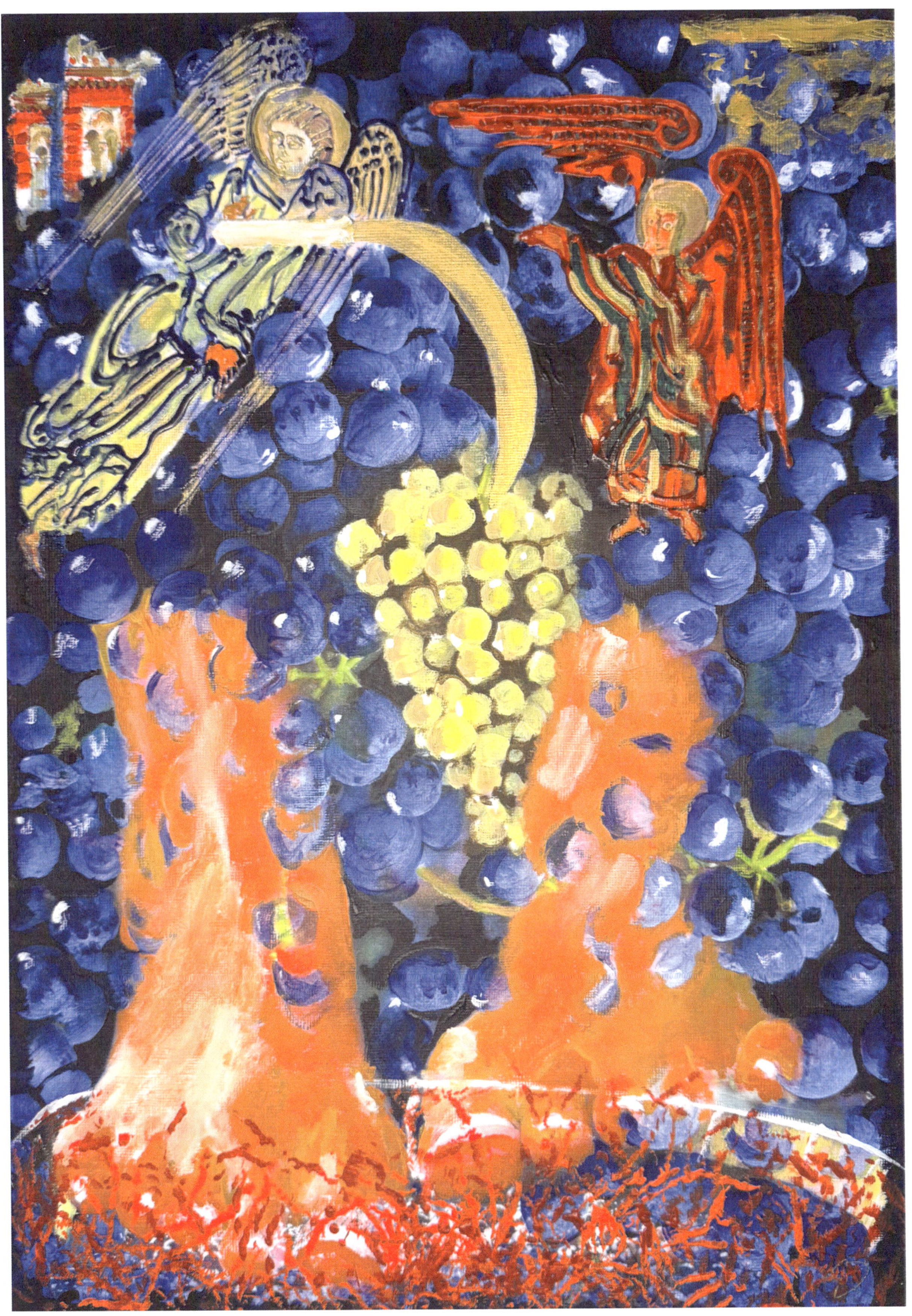

Outside the City

"Outside the City" reminds us of Hebrews 13:13 and the significance of the cross. It also takes us back to Leviticus and Deuteronomy, where anything unholy or related to death was kept outside the camp.

Which city is in view? Most commentators think it is the New Jerusalem. However, if it is applied to Jesus, then Jerusalem in the time of writing could also be in view.

In my painting, I depict this ambiguity by portraying the current Jerusalem wall alongside the symbolic image I use previously to represent the New Jerusalem, or the church, in my work. This then could represent redemption, with the blood of Jesus metaphorically covering the whole world: 1,600 stadia is the product of 4 x 4 x 100, which represents the entire known world.

In the context of letters written to the churches, this verse is therefore a revelation, first, of the work of Christ outside the city on behalf of all those who believe in Him.

14: [20]And the winepress was trodden outside the city, and blood flowed from the winepress, as high as a horse's bridle, for a distance of about one thousand six hundred stadia.

In the Val-Dieu image below, the New Jerusalem scene is clearly related to the future. I am not sure why the beast is included, as the text says nothing about him, and I find it an unhelpful addition.

Secondly, this vision could signify the terrible judgement that awaits those who reject Christ, in which case it occurs outside the New Jerusalem. If so, it must be taken proleptically, or as an introduction to what will be described in more detail in the revelation still to come?

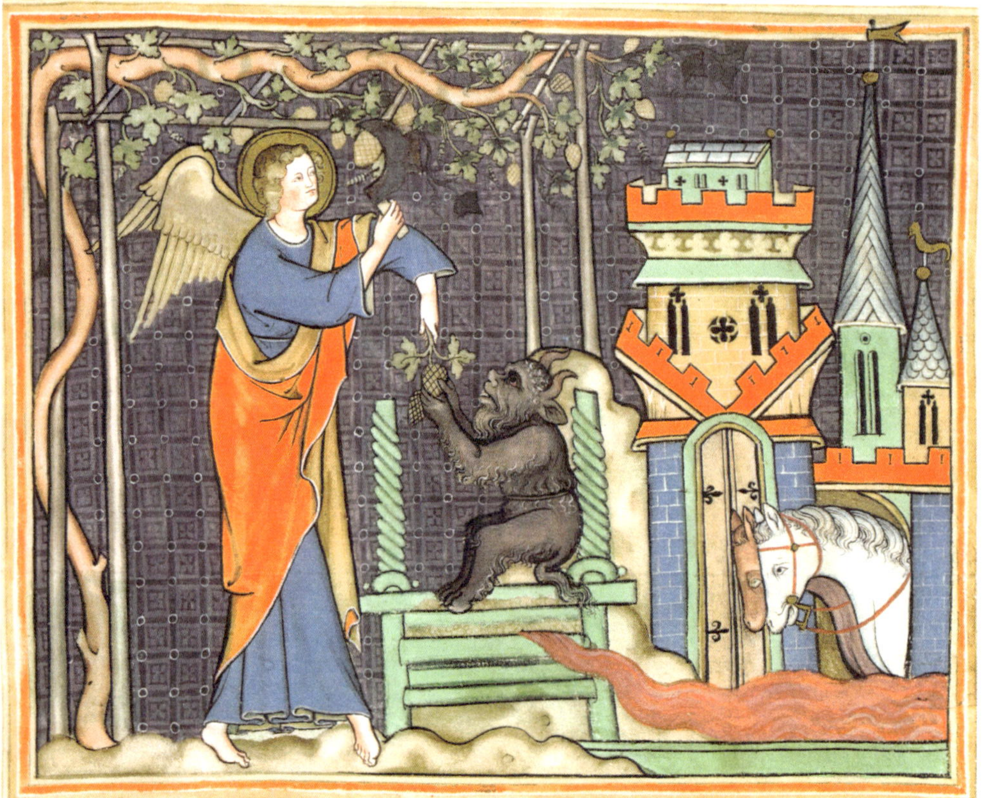

It becomes clear that for God's salvation to achieve final justice, it appears always linked with judgement.

At this point the fate of the beasts and of their powers, and of those who follow them, are not yet revealed.

Nevertheless, what appears already clear is that Jesus is at the centre. And that every faithful believer may find him or herself in that unholy place "outside the city". The churches have been encouraged to persevere and to endure in perseverance ... but this chapter of Revelation closes with a dire image of judgement!

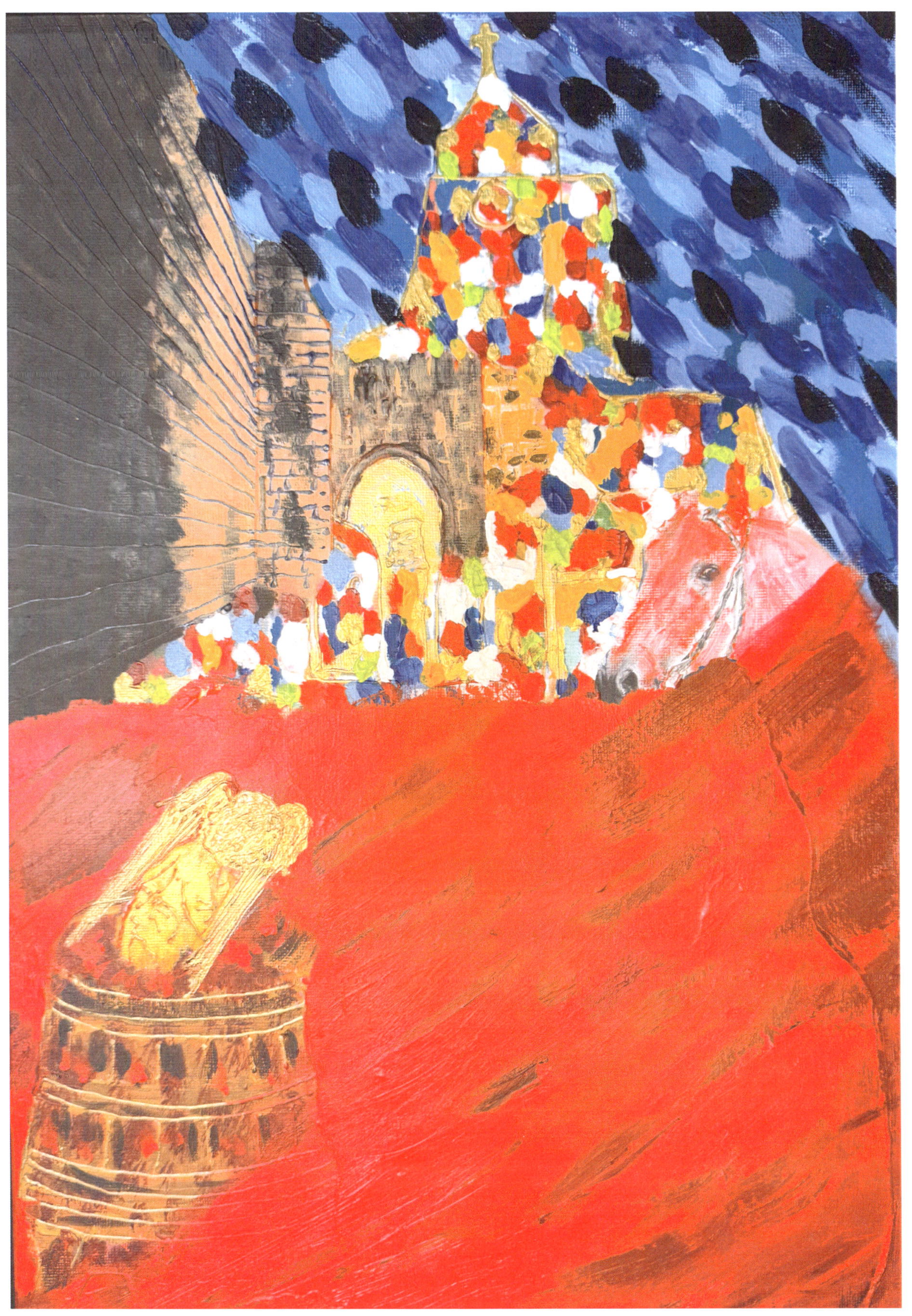

My Understanding of Endurance and War

The seventh trumpet has sounded in heaven (11:15), beginning the series of visions that reveal the mystery of God as prophesied in 10:7. However, John has not yet discovered what the third woe entails (11:14), and he has not yet seen 11:8 being enacted: the wrath of the nations destroying those who destroy the earth, and servants who fear God's name receiving their reward. Having been introduced to the contents of the open scroll in Revelation 11, John now sees more and more detail.

Two of the three major signs are introduced and named quickly in Revelation 12, with a further one appearing in Revelation 15 and being discussed in Volume 5. These signs introduce the main characters – the woman, the dragon and the child – as well as the major heavenly battle and how their interactions reverberate through earthly time into God's heavenly, spiritual "time".

Revelation 13 next introduces two more demonic beasts operating on earth, as well as their followers. Then, in Revelation 14, the Lamb and the Son of Man appear with the Lamb's followers, showing John (and us) again that what happens on earth is linked in reality with heavenly events. All occur according to God's timeline, which does not necessarily align with ours. I am convinced that it is futile to use "time" as a tool for understanding Revelation. The ancients with their suprahistorical and allegorical interpretations were not altogether wrong, in my view (for example the apt quote by Caesarius in the Epigraph to this book).

Revelation 12 to 14 was of course first written to "the seven churches". Christ is not silent in their suffering. He acts by revealing to the suffering why they are facing such demanding challenges. At the same time he shows them, and those who are not (yet?) suffering, how to recognise their enemy and how to overcome him! Christ points out their lack of love and their laziness, but He also points out satanic attacks from outside – the synagogue of Satan and the throne of Satan – as well as from inside – Balaam and Jezebel learning the "deep things" of Satan. The temptation for the churches to conform to the world is set in the context of such satanic attacks and leads to wake-up calls in Sardis, pressure to endure in Philadelphia and an invitation to communion with Christ. Two very strong imperatives appear in 13:10 and 14:12. The saints are urged to persevere in endurance and faith. I believe the main purpose of these chapters is exactly that: to urge believers, including us, to recognise our enemy while preparing to endure faith-fully in the battle for the victory on earth.

Why must the churches endure? Because there is war! The text illustrates this with the first sign: a woman in labour. She represents Eve, Mary and all the other women who have given life before and after them. At her most vulnerable time, the second sign appears: the ancient serpent, who is the devil and Satan that leads the whole world astray. Satan starts the fight by sweeping down one third of the stars and preparing himself to devour the child. This "sweep" of his tail portrays an aggressive, proud move and may refer to a previous battle. John is given no more detail or explanation, but he sees that the child, despite this vicious threat, is convincingly rescued and swept up to the throne of God. This aggressive and decisive counter-move, which places the child on the throne of God, is widely interpreted as representing Christ's "enthronement": the child who is the King.

When did this war between the woman and the serpent start? Some commentators think it refers to Christ's birth. I prefer Caird's interpretation, namely Jesus' crucifixion and ascension. What is clear is that He rules as Messiah in the manner described in Psalm 2, with a "rod of iron". His power is not merely "soft".

After the child is saved, the woman flees. The phrase "1,260 days" recurs again and again, though slightly differently expressed, and it refers to a period of time. It is generally interpreted as referring to the time between the ascension of Jesus and His "second coming". Some interpret it as a more literal time before the actual Parousia. I think both are possible, as long as we interpret the number to have symbolical meaning, more than being a precise prediction of a fixed number of hours and minutes. It then represents three-and-a-half years, which signifies a split number seven, for war breaks things! Moved by these dramatic and disturbing visions, are we urged too, with the help of the Spirit, to discern what time we are living in so as to act accordingly?

Next John is shown a war in heaven, in which the angel Michael represents God as He fights alongside His angels against the devil and his angels. The devil is defeated and thrown down to the earth, just as he had earlier thrown God's angels down to earth. A voice from heaven proclaims the victor: "The accuser of our brothers and sisters has been thrown down." However, an extraordinary revelation shows John more: it was the church, through Christ, who won that victory! "They triumphed over him by the blood of the Lamb and by the word of their testimony. Rejoice, you heavens! And woe to the earth and the sea, for the devil has come down to you, filled with fury because he knows he has little time." The devil, in response, intensifies his war on earth against the woman. But God gives her "the gift of wings and flight". Earth also takes the woman's side and swallows whatever the devil throws at it. The devil, frustrated in his pursuit of the woman, expands his war and declares enmity against all her offspring!

Our current world political situation, with relentlessly destructive wars continuing unabated, most notably for me in Ukraine and Gaza, put flesh on the war described in the biblical text and the hatred that drives it, as well as the hatred it leaves in its wake, possibly for many generations. Amazingly, God has not withdrawn following the great rejoicing in heaven to celebrate Satan's defeat there, insulating Himself from the dire realities on earth. For the battle continues, but now on earth, where victory will again be achieved by enduring believers!

What kind of war was this? Some see the heavenly war as a metaphor for a legal battle in heaven (Caird). While I agree with this interpretation, I wonder if it rules out a literal battle, involving the removal of one of God's former councillors from heaven to earth, as other commentators suggest? Opinions vary, also on when this war took place. Some suggest it started before the Fall (Minear), others at the Fall in Genesis 3, and still others (like König) that it began with the earthly life and death of Jesus. I believe that the war in heaven has been fought, and that the war on earth is now continuing between the beasts and the church. It is primarily a spiritual war, but it can manifest itself in all areas of life: war against the self, the world and/or the devil, as our forefathers rightly formulated. Revelation 13 and 14 make it clear that we are fighting "the powers of darkness" (Ephesians 6).

I found studying and painting these chapters very challenging, and I was very aware of the spiritual nature of this battle. Spending nine months reading about and studying these evil creatures showed me the darkness we may have to endure. It is a messy and dark world, and we find the same within ourselves. These chapters address the origins of this conflict and explain why we find it so difficult. They explain why our Christian lives are so easily compromised and what powers we are up against.

Satan summons two helpers: one from the sea and one from the earth. They are beasts. One is in Satan's exact image, and the other is in the image of a lamb that parodies the enthroned child Lamb. These beasts are loosely based on OT images of Leviathan (Psalm 74:10–17) and Behemoth. What matters is that though they appear to be created beasts, they are revealed to be demonic. Many commentators describe these creatures by what they represent. But here that approach seems wrong. Later in the Book of Revelation we discover what they may represent, but here only one aspect is important: that they are evil and demonic, and work together through force, lies and fake news! They use miracles, statues, technology and anything else to draw people in to worship the beast!

Are they the Antichrist? That title is never used in Revelation. Perhaps it is wise for us to not use it either. While the beasts are clearly anti-Christian, we should not get distracted from the main point: they are demonic and at war with God's people because of our allegiance to the Child King. We oppose and resist these evil beasts in our daily lives!

The Sea beast is viewed with wonder by onlookers, and the fact that his fatal wound was healed is mentioned repeatedly – to parody Christ's resurrection – and it is a clear reference also to the original battle in Genesis 3 (Minear). The beast blasphemes against God and heaven and becomes so successful that the inhabitants of the earth follow him. He is given power to wage war and conquer those who follow the heavenly Lamb. Many are deceived by the lies and deceptions, including, it seems, some within the church. Exclusion from privilege if you are not a follower of the beast is a recurring theme, in society, economics, politics and so on, and even in the church. Everyone is forced to be marked with the name of the Beast, 666, the number and mark of imperfection.

In Revelation 14, the Lamb of God is in Zion, surrounded by the 144,000 first fruits of all God's people – those who had already been martyred by the time the Book of Revelation was written. They hear a new song and learn it so that they can sing along. They are marked with the name of God on their foreheads. Clearly, these marks on hands and foreheads are symbolic, while we note that there is no mention of "unmarked" people!

The vision then moves from war to judgement and resolution through six angels and the Son of Man, followed by seven final and complete judgements (Revelation 15). The first three angels announce the good news: the everlasting gospel first, then the destruction of Babylon (we know nothing more about her yet, except that she will be destroyed), and finally the destruction of the beasts and their followers, who despite their great success will meet a terrible end, described in horrifying detail in order to both warn the churches, and encourage them to endure.

The second beatitude of Revelation appears here: "Blessed are the dead who die in the Lord from now on." It seems that "from now on" indicates a period of time, perhaps after the crucifixion? Then the Son of Man will appear to harvest the grain, referring to believers in the context of the gospel. The harvest of the 144,000 was the first fruit of this harvest! An angel emerges from the heavenly temple and the presence of God to announce the time for the harvest to begin. Two more angels appear, to harvest those with the mark of the beast. There is one vine, reminding us of Jesus and Israel. Is its fruit being trampled "outside the city" to remind us of Jesus' crucifixion? The blood may signify the blood of Jesus and/or the blood of those who did not repent. The two harvests are both metaphors that can be proleptic, looking to the future, or as referring to the harvest that the church is already part of (in John 5). They also remind us of the "two resurrections" mentioned there: one to life and the other to condemnation.

The response to the second beatitude, "Blessed are the dead who die in the Lord from now on" is the Spirit's yes, "they will rest from their labour, for their deeds will follow them." Those who endured to the point of paying with their lives will not have suffered and endured in vain.

Visual Meditation 5

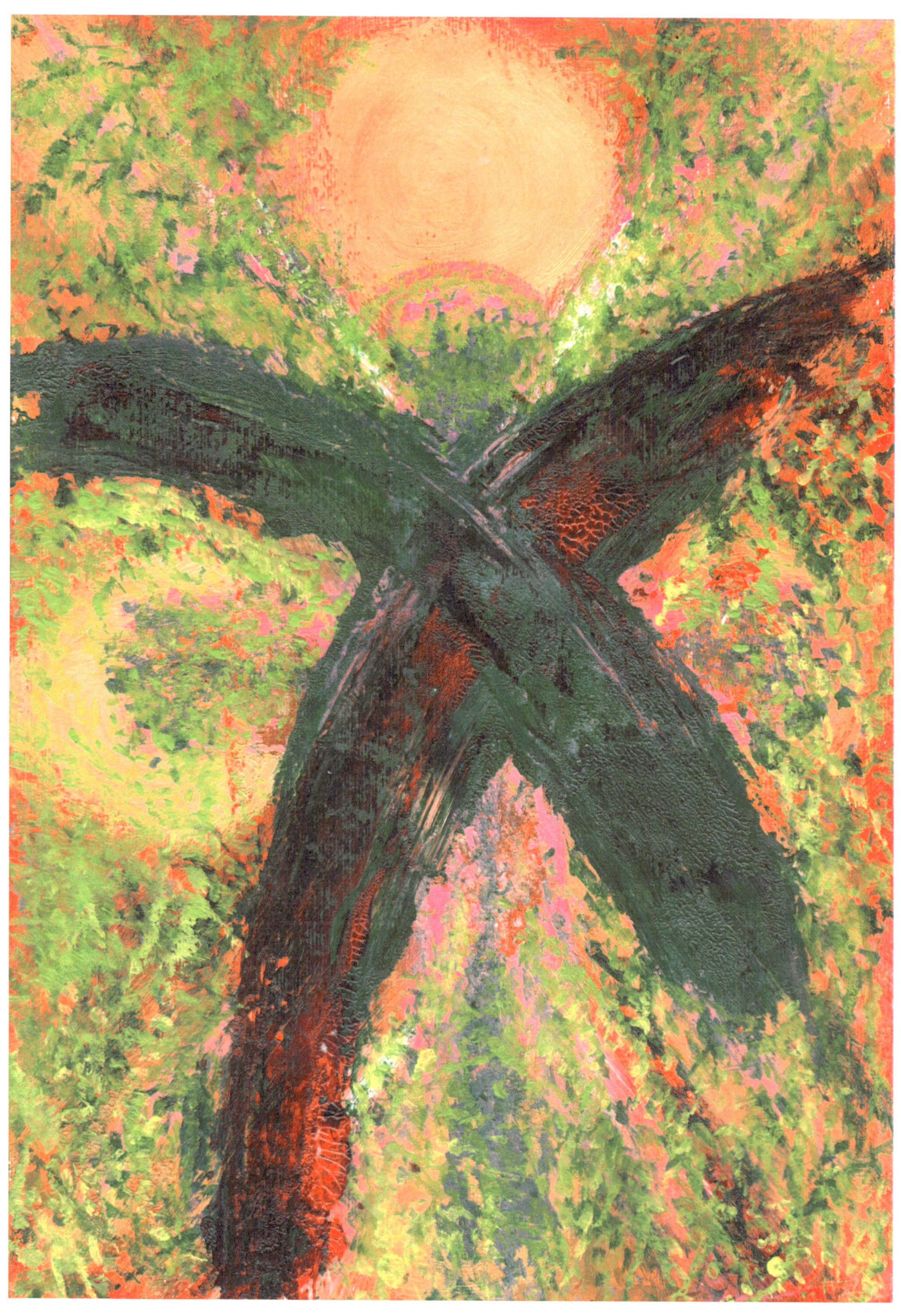

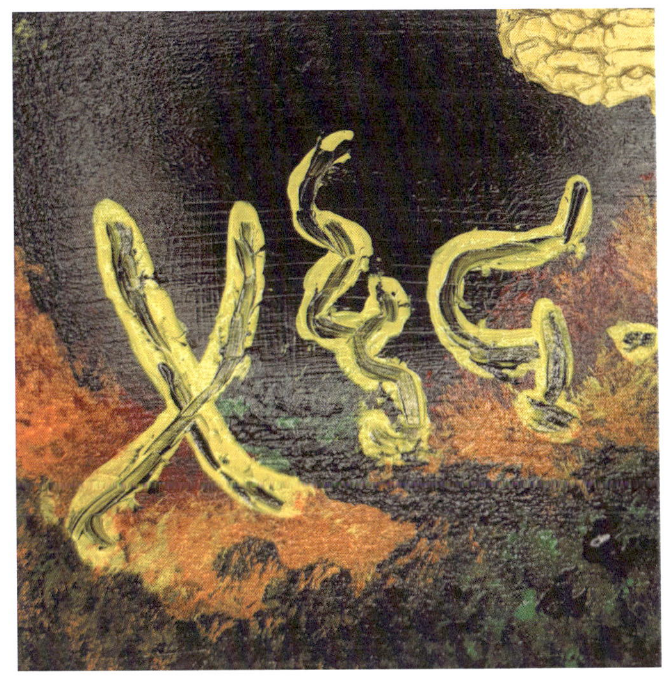

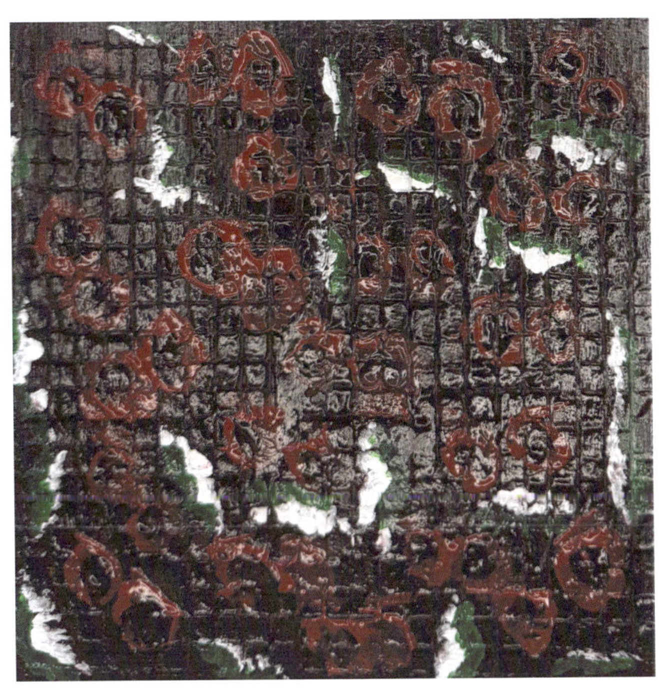

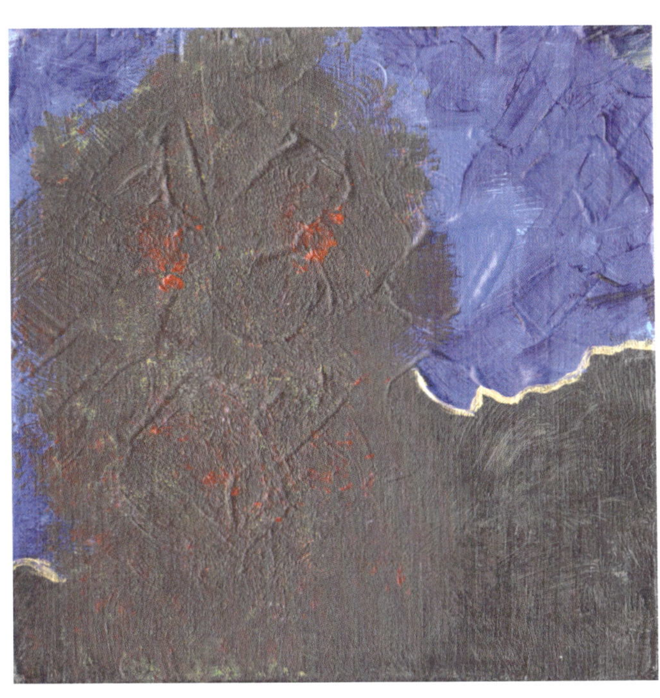

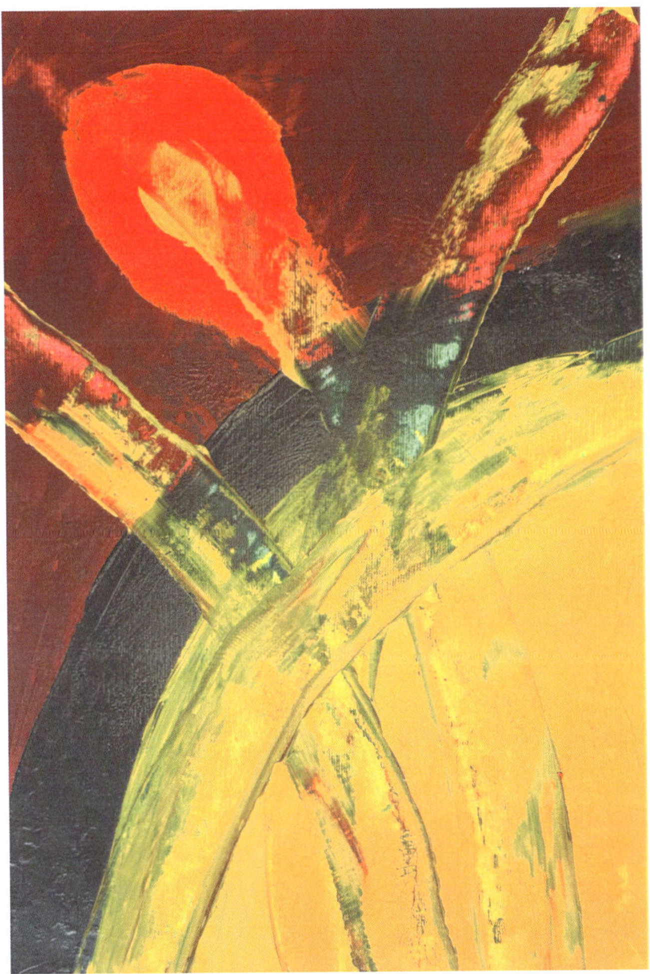

Reading and List of Illustrations

Select Further Reading on Medieval MSS

Emmerson, R. K. *Apocalypse Illuminated: the visual exegesis of Revelation in medieval illustrated manuscripts.* University Park, PA: The Pennsylvania State University Press, 2018.

McKitterick, D. J. *The Trinity Apocalypse.* Trinity College, Cambridge: Ms.R.16.2. London: British Library, 2005.

O'Hear, Natasha and Anthony. *Picturing the Apocalypse: the book of Revelation in the arts over two millennia.* Oxford: OUP, 2017.

O'Hear, Natasha F. H. *Contrasting Images of the Book of Revelation in Late Medieval and Early Modern Art: a case study in visual exegesis.* Oxford: Oxford University Press, 2013.

Van der Meer, Frederick. *Apocalypse: visions from the book of Revelation in western art.* NY: Alpine Fine Arts Collection, 1978.

Williams, John. *The Illustrated Beatus: a corpus of illustrations of the commentary on the Apocalypse.* London: Miller, 1994.

Illuminated and illustrated Apocalypses

Dürer, *Apocalypse* [Dürer], 1498. The complete series of 15 woodcuts appear full-page in my copy of Van der Meer's *Apocalypse.*

The Apocalypse of 1313. Besseyre, Marianne, and Marie-Thérèse Gousset, 2008. Copyright © M/ Moleiro Editor.

The Getty Apocalypse. Described in the Morgan title above. MS LUDWIG III 1, 1255–60 (Getty Museum); previously known as the Dyson Perrins Apocalypse. Creative Commons Licence CC01.0.

The Morgan Beatus. See Williams title below.

The Rylands Beatus. Manchester: The John Rylands University Library, Latin MS 8, 1175. Copyright © The University of Manchester, 2021.

The Trier Apocalypse. Trier, Germany: Stadtbibliothek, MS 31, approx. AD 500.

The Trinity Apocalypse MS R.16.2, 1260. https://mss-cat.trin.cam. ac.uk/Manuscript/R.16.2

Hommel-Steenbakkers, Nelly de, A. M. Koldeweij, Miró Mónica and Ruth Koenig. *Flemish Apocalypse (Apokalipsis in Dietsche).* Barcelona: Moleiro, 2005.

Liśkiewicz, Izabela, Richard Kenneth Emmerson, Peter Kidd, Britt Boler Hunter, *Picture Book of the Life of St John and the Apocalypse.* Barcelona: M. Moleiro Editor S.A., 2020.

Miró Vinaixa, Mònica. *The Val-Dieu Apocalypse.* Barcelona: M. Moleiro, 2020.

Moleiro, Manuel, Anne Barton de Mayor, Nigel Morgan, Suzanne Lewis, Aires Nascimento, Michelle P. Brown and Raquel Somoano, *Gulbenkian Apocalypse / Apocalipsis Gulbenkian.* Barcelona: Moleiro, 2019.

Williams, J. A. *A Spanish Apocalypse: the Morgan Beatus manuscript.* NY: Braziller, 1991.

Paintings by Pieter Kwant

Paintings by Other Artists

8 The Serpent's battle against the Son of the woman. Folios 147v-148r

10 Detail Woman clothed with the Sun, Folio 143v. From the *Rylands Beatus*. Copyright ©The University of Manchester, 2021. Used with permission.

11 The Dragon and the Beast. Folio 040r. From *Trier*, Germany: Stadtbibliothek, MS 31. In public domain.

11 Woman and Dragon. Folio 029v From *The Bamberg Apocalypse*. MS Bibl. 140, Bamberg, Staatsbibliothek. In public domain.

12 The seven-headed dragon appears before the woman in the sun whose child is taken up to heaven; the woman in the wilderness. Trinity Apocalypse. Folio13r. From the *Trinity Apocalypse*. Used with permission of the Masters and fellows of Trinity College, Cambridge.

12 The Great Dragon appears; The Child of the Woman in the Sun is taken up to Heaven; The woman departs to the wilderness. Folio 20r

13 The Temple of Heaven, the Woman of the Sun and the seven headed Dragon. Folio 29r. From the *Gulbenkian Apocalypse*. Barcelona: Moleiro, 2019. Used with permission.

14 The vision of the woman and the dragon. Apocalypse of 1313 Folio 35r From the *Apocalypse of 1313*. Copyright ©M. Moleiro Editor, 2015.

11 The Temple in Heaven; the Appearance of the Woman in the Sun and the Seven-Headed Red Dragon; The Woman in the Wilderness. Folio 19r.

14 Woman harassed by the Dragon Folio 20v, register 1. War in Heaven Folio 20v, register 2 12

14 The Temple in Heaven and the woman in the sun and the seven-headed Dragon Folio 13r 12

14 Woman facing Dragon and war in heaven page 23v From *Block book: Die Urausgaben Der Holländischen Apokalypse Und Biblia Pauperum*. Munchen: Prestel, 1961

15 The pregnant Woman; the Dragon; the child carried to the Lord; the earth swallowing the water; the stars swept down by the Dragon's tail. From Albrecht Dürer; the complete series of 15 woodcuts 1498

15 Die Sechzehend Figur, *The Luther Bible of 1534*, Folio CXCII

16 The woman in the Sun appears in Heaven, Folio19v

18 Anneke Kaai, *Woman and Dragon*, page 31(Half the image), *Apocalypse*, 1992

20 Hans Feibusch, of the Woman clothed with the Sun. *The Revelation of Saint John the Divine: with Lithographs*. London: Collins, 1900

22 The Temple in Heaven and the woman in the sun and the seven-headed Dragon Folio 13r

24 The Serpent's battle against the Son of the woman. Folios 147v-148r

26 Voice in Heaven promises Salvation. Folio 21v, register 1

28 The Dragon casts out a Flood at the Woman. Folio 20v

30 The Dragon, the seven-headed beast from the sea and the false prophet. Folio 14r

32 Worship of the Beast from the Sea and the Dragon. Folio 22r

34 Die Sichtzehend Figur, *The Luther Bible of 1534*, Folio CXCIII

36 The Beast from the Land brings down Fire from Heaven and orders the worship of the Beast of the Sea. Folio 23r

38 The Beast from the Land orders the killing of those who refuse to worship the statue of the Beast from the Sea. Folio 23v

40 The False Prophet kills those who refuse to worship the image of the Beast and orders that All Men should be marked. Folio 25v

42 The Lamb on Mount Zion. Folio 164r

44 The new canticle sung by the voices before the Lamb and the throne of God. Folio 26v

46 The First Angel saying "Fear the Lord." Folio 25r

48 The Second Angel proclaims the Fall of Babylon. Folio 25v

50 The Third Angel: The Judgement of those who worship the Beast. Folio 28r

54 Blessed are the dead who die in the Lord. Folio 26v

56 The Winepress of God's wrath. Folio 178v. From *Spanish Apocalypse: The Morgan Beatus Manuscript*. NY: Brazier, 1991

58 The Adoration of the Lamb, the Fall of Babylon, the harvesting of the earth. Folio 15r

60 The angel gathers the grapes and the blood from the winepress of God's wrath. Folio 28r

8, 24, 42 From the *Silos Beatus*. MS11695 (The British Library, London). Copyright ©M. Moleiro, S.A., 2019

12, 16, 40, 44, 50 From the *Dyson Perrins Apocalypse*. MSLudwig III 1 (Getty Museum). Creative Commons Licence CC01.0

14, 28, 32, 36, 38, 46, 48, 54, 60 From the *Val-Dieu Apocalypse*. Barcelona: M. Moleiro, 2020

14, 22, 30, 58 From *Flemish Apocalypse (Apokalipsis in Dietsche)*. Barcelona: M. Moleiro, 2020

14,26 From *Picture book of the Life of St John and the Apocalypse*. Barcelona: M. Moleiro, S.A., 2020

Table of Contents

www.ingramcontent.com/pod-product-compliance
Lightning Source LLC
LaVergne TN
LVRC090924100826
845154LV00013B/158